LEONARDO DA VINCI
HIS LIFE AND HIS PICTURES

THE UNIVERSITY OF CHICAGO PRESS · CHICAGO

Agent: THE CAMBRIDGE UNIVERSITY PRESS · LONDON

PLATE I

LEONARDO DA VINCI. A CARTOON, THE VIRGIN AND CHILD
AND ST. ANNE. ROYAL ACADEMY, LONDON

LEONARDO DA VINCI
HIS LIFE AND HIS PICTURES

BY R. LANGTON DOUGLAS

UNIVERSITY OF CHICAGO PRESS · CHICAGO

ND
623
L5
D68

11/2/44 Leonard

025068

TO
PERCY S. STRAUS
1876-1944

A LOYAL FRIEND
A GOOD CITIZEN
A FINE CONNOISSEUR OF THE ARTS

PREFACE

SO MANY books have been published on Leonardo that I feel that I ought to offer some justification for adding to their number. My chief reason for writing this book is that I believe that I have something to say about the artist and his works that is both new and true.

In the first three chapters of the book, I give an account of the life of Leonardo, drawing special attention to those elements of his early environment that had a lasting effect on the development of his artistic personality.

In the fourth chapter, which is entitled "Melzi's Heritage," I describe the collection of manuscripts, drawings, and cartoons that Leonardo bequeathed to his faithful friend and pupil, Francesco Melzi, and narrate briefly the subsequent history of the more important items in that collection.

In the fifth chapter, I discuss those methods of art criticism that have been in vogue in the last seventy years, and endeavor to show how far they have helped, and in what respects they have retarded, the development of our knowledge of Leonardo's works.

In the seven remaining chapters, I give an account of Leonardo's paintings in their chronological order, and state my reasons for attributing to him certain pictures which some critics have not, as yet, included in their lists of his works. I strive to show what it was that he aimed at when he began to paint each of his more important pictures. I also endeavor to put on record what I myself have felt when contemplating them.

It has not been difficult to give to the book a certain unity: with Leonardo, more than with most men, it is obvious that the child was father of the man.

This book would never have been finished but for the constant help and encouragement I have received from my wife. I wish, too, to acknowledge the debt that I owe to Dr. William Valentiner for placing at my disposal his fine collection of photographs of Leonardo's works, and for permitting me to publish his recent discovery of a missing panel of the predella of the "Madonna di Piazza." I desire to express my gratitude to Professor Lionello Venturi for lending me books from his library and to Professor W. Suida for assistance when I was collecting material for illustrations. I wish also to thank the librarians of the Metropolitan Museum, as well as the staff of the Frick Art Reference Library, for their patient and unstinted services. Miss Rosalie B. Green has read my manuscript, and has made helpful suggestions in regard to the not unimportant matters of punctuation and emphasis. For other good offices I am much indebted to the Director of the University of Chicago Press and to Miss Mary D. Alexander.

In writing this book, I have felt that it was my duty to give my reasons for disagreeing with much that Mr. Bernhard Berenson has written on the subject of Leonardo. But it would be ungracious of me not to acknowledge here my own indebtedness to this distinguished critic for the valuable additions that he has made in the course of half a century to our knowledge of Italian painting.

Finally, I wish to acknowledge my debt to Professor Ulrich Middeldorf, who has given me invaluable help in preparing this book for the press. He must not, however, be held accountable for any of the statements or opinions that are recorded in it. For these, the author alone is responsible.

R. LANGTON DOUGLAS

TABLE OF CONTENTS

LIST OF PLATES

xi

CHAPTER I

LEONARDO'S LIFE
1452-78

LEONARDO DA VINCI was born on April 15, 1452,[1] in the house of his grandfather at Vinci, a small town situated above the Arno Valley, on the slopes of Monte Albano. He was the illegitimate son of a young notary, Ser Piero d'Antonio da Vinci, by a girl named Caterina, who subsequently became the wife of Accattabriga di Piero da Vinci. In the same year that Leonardo was born, Ser Piero, the fifth of a line of notaries, married a daughter of a noble Florentine family, Albiera di Giovanni Amadori. The future artist's father was a successful man, and became, in course of time, the head of his profession. Existing records show that no other notary of Florence had so many clients.

Leonardo passed his early childhood at Vinci, at the home of his grandparents, amidst the sights and sounds of a Tuscan countryside. Here, as a little boy, he developed that keen interest in nature that remained with him throughout his long life. In fact, it pained him so to cause hurt to any living thing that he became a vegetarian.[2] The earliest of his drawings that is known to us is a rural landscape, a view of the Arno Valley, which is dated 1473.[3]

A great deal of superfluous pity has been bestowed on the

---

[1] E. Moeller, "Der Geburtstag des Leonardo da Vinci," *Jahrbuch d. Preuss. Kunstsamml.* (1939), pp. 71–75. Moeller publishes a statement written by Antonio da Vinci which reveals the grandfather's satisfaction at the birth of his first grandchild and records the fact that several leading citizens assisted at the baptismal ceremony.

[2] This information is contained in a letter, written in January, 1515, by the Florentine traveler, Andrea Corsali, to Giuliano de'Medici. See G. B. Ramusio, *Primo Volume delle Navigazioni e Viaggi*, etc. (Venice, 1550), fol. 194v; also Luca Beltrami, *Documenti e Memorie riguardanti la Vita e le Opere di Leonardo da Vinci* (Milan: Fratelli Treves, 1919), p. 145.

[3] B. Berenson, *The Drawings of the Florentine Painters* (London: John Murray, 1903), Vol. II, p. 57, No. 1017; also H. Bodmer, *Leonardo: Des Meisters Gemälde und Zeichnungen* ("Klassiker der Kunst" Series [Stuttgart, 1931]), pp. iii and 378. See Pl. I.

young Leonardo by imaginative writers who had, it would appear, an imperfect acquaintance with the social history of Italy in the age of the Renaissance, and no exact knowledge of the domestic conditions that helped to mold the character of Piero da Vinci's eldest son.

He has been portrayed as an ill-used illegitimate child whose presence in the family was bitterly resented by his stepmother, and by his father's lawful offspring. Without doubt the creative imagination of every writer who drew a portrait of this kind of the child Leonardo, was powerfully affected by his knowledge of social life in some respectable community in a later period of history. These biographers ignore the fact that in Italy, in the fifteenth century, it was no very unusual thing for an illegitimate child to be taken into his father's family and to be accorded the same privileges as the other children. In that age, there were infants born out of wedlock who, after they came to manhood, became the founders of dynasties; whilst other bastards attained high positions in the Church, and in society.

Caterina Sforza, for example, a natural daughter of Galeazzo Sforza, was received into the ducal family at Milan by Galeazzo's wife, Bona of Savoy, and became, in later life, the sovereign head of an Italian state and is known to history as the heroic defender of Forlì.

Even so serious a writer as Sirén seems to have allowed his imagination to run riot in describing the early life of "the little Leonardo." "The illegitimate child," he tells us, in a passage that is full of pathos, "found little happiness at home. . . . . In the course of the father's third and fourth marriages, the family circle (now removed to Florence) rapidly increased, making life at home almost unendurable to Leonardo. His stepbrothers and sisters and even his father seem always to have regarded him as 'the illegitimate one,' a kind of intruder, against whom they might freely vent their spite and bitterness." "These impressions of childhood," Sirén concludes, "cannot have failed to have influenced Leonardo's future development."[4]

---

[4] O. Sirén, *Leonardo da Vinci, the Artist and the Man* (New Haven and London, 1916), p. 4.

Now this picture of Leonardo's childhood is purely imaginary. He was, for nearly a quarter of a century, the only child of a father who was, Vasari tells us, "an excellent parent." It was not until Leonardo was twenty-four years of age, a practising artist and a member of the Florentine Guild of Painters, that Antonio, Piero's second son, was born; and the artist was only twenty-eight years old when his father's third child, Giuliano, saw the light. He was already a middle-aged man, and had gained world-wide fame by his "Last Supper," before his elder sister, Violante, could have caught a glimpse of him. How, then, could the "petty spite and bitterness" of his brothers and sisters have rendered his childhood "unendurable," and "have influenced Leonardo's future development"?

The fact is that Leonardo had all the advantages and disadvantages of an only child in a well-to-do family. He was good-looking, and had unusual physical strength and a quick intelligence. It cannot be doubted that he was a spoiled child, the idol of his grandmother, and perhaps even of his childless step-mother. After the fashion of spoiled children, it became, no doubt, a habit with him to play eagerly with some new toy, and, tiring of it quickly, to throw it down and take up another, being full of curiosity, restless, never satisfied. "Dimmi se mai fu fatta alcuna cosa."—"Tell me if anything was ever finished."[5] —This became the *bourdon* of his life, inscribed by him, on his drawings and manuscripts. For he continued to be a spoiled child as long as he lived. No man ever had bestowed on him more gifts or more opportunities for using them. Did he tire of what he was doing, did he come up against some unexpected difficulty, there were always at hand a lot of things that he could do, and do effectively if only he exercised some steadfastness, some persistency; but these virtues he did not possess. His recurrent failures were not due to dilatoriness but to inconstancy, the inconstancy of a spoiled child. "Variable and unstable," says Vasari, "he set himself to learn many things, and then abandoned them after he had begun them." Leonardo

---

[5] J. P. and Irma A. Richter, *The Literary Works of Leonardo da Vinci* (Oxford University Press, 1939), II, 343.

was the victim of a fickle sincerity. And this failing grew with the years.

Vasari tells us that the child soon revealed a love for drawing. His father, who was a friend of Verrocchio, took some of the boy's sketches to show them to the artist. Verrocchio, like Ser Piero himself, was in favor with the ruling family of the Republic, having been appointed, when still young, the official artist of the Medici. "Andrea was amazed," Vasari tells us, "when he saw the extraordinary beginnings of Leonardo, and exhorted Ser Piero that he should make the boy study drawing. Whereupon the father arranged with Leonardo that he should go to the workshop of Andrea; which Leonardo did with extraordinary willingness."

There is no good reason for doubting these statements of Vasari. Leonardo must, it would appear, have shown at an early age what his vocation was, and what he wished to do. Had he not done so, he would probably have been destined to follow the hereditary profession of this family of notaries, of which then, and for several years afterwards, he was the only male child. But Leonardo, although he was a boy of exceptional intelligence, and had a rich and ambitious father, received but the ordinary elementary education given, in that age, to boys of the upper and middle classes, that is to say he learned to read, to write, and to use the abacus. He had at that time, it seems, no ambitions to become a man of letters, or a scientific student. He was not eager to study more of mathematics than simple arithmetic. Nor was he anxious to read the Greek and Roman classics. These desires came to him in later life. He wanted, in fact, to be an artist.

That he was allowed extraordinary freedom, even in his early years when at school, is shown by the fact that he acquired the habit of writing from right to left; notwithstanding that, like many left-handed persons, he was, in a measure, ambidextrous, and could have learned to write freely with his right hand. The young Leonardo found it easier to write in this most unusual manner; and, being an attractive child with a strong will, he had his way.

In Florence, in the fifteenth century, boys as a rule were apprenticed to a trade or craft when they completed their thirteenth year. It seems, therefore, that the young Leonardo entered Verrocchio's studio in 1465. There can, as we have said, be no valid reason for doubting that it was in or about that year that he began his training as an artist. The fact that he is not mentioned as living under Verrocchio's roof before 1476 counts for nothing. Not all of that master's numerous apprentices and assistants "lived in": Credi certainly did not. Leonardo's father, Ser Piero, had a thriving business in Florence and had a residence there. It is true that, in his grandmother's tax return of 1469, Leonardo is included in the list of those who were then living at her house at Vinci. But the statement only implies that, at the time the return was signed, Leonardo was on a visit to his old home.[6] This fact becomes clear to us when we note that, in the year that it was made, Ser Piero was official notary to the Republic of Florence with a large private practice in the city, that he had an apartment in the Palazzo del Podestà, and that he rented a house in the Via delle Prestanze, now the Via de' Gondi.[7] But Ser Piero had, also, like most well-to-do Florentines, a villa in the country, on his native soil.

Leonardo entered the studio of Andrea del Verrocchio at an early age. This great teacher did as much as can be done by a mentor to mold the character of an intelligent pupil. Verrocchio was a goldsmith and a sculptor, an architect and a painter, a musician and a student of those sciences that are the handmaids of painting, but that ought not to be permitted to dominate a creative artist. It was to Verrocchio that Leonardo owed the development of his genius, his mastery of many arts, his universal curiosity and love of knowledge. But in one important particular he did not follow his master: he did not regard sculpture as an art of equal importance to painting, nor did he devote his best energies to that art. In spite of all temporary infidelities—and they were many—he was always

[6] L. Beltrami, op. cit., p. 2.

[7] G. Poggi, Leonardo da Vinci, La Vita di Giorgio Vasari Nuovamente Commentata e Illustrata, etc. (Florence, 1919), p. 2.

loyal *au fond* to his first love. He was, throughout his career, primarily a painter.

It was in the year 1472 that Leonardo became a member of the Compagnia di San Luca, the Florentine Guild of Artists, that is to say in the same year in which Andrea della Robbia was its *Camarlingo*. The pen drawing of the Arno Valley made in the following year reveals that the artist had behind him a considerable period of training and practice.

According to Vasari, Leonardo, when still young, assisted his master by painting an angel in a picture of the "Baptism of Christ," an altarpiece which Verrocchio had been commissioned to make by the Frati di Vallombrosa, for their church at San Salvi in Florence. This statement of the Aretine biographer is confirmed by a contemporary of Leonardo, Francesco Albertini, in his *Memoriale*, as well as by the picture itself.[8] Vasari adds that Verrocchio, after seeing it, never touched a brush again. This is clearly an exaggeration. For not only did Verrocchio continue to accept commissions for pictures, he also became the instructor of the greatest painters of the day, numbering amongst his pupils Botticelli, Domenico Ghirlandajo, and Perugino, as well as such minor artists as Botticini and Lorenzo di Credi.

The subject of all others that occupied most constantly Leonardo's imagination, throughout his career as a painter, was that of the divine Mother and her Child. "A feeling for maternity," says Pater, "is always characteristic of Leonardo." And it was as a painter of small Madonnas that he became famous throughout Christendom, not only at the Papal Court, at Milan, and at Mantua, but also at the courts of France, Germany, and Hungary. His first painting of this subject is, we believe, the little "Madonna and Child" that was in the Dreyfus Collection. For in it Leonardo follows Verrocchio more closely—both in the landscape and in the lines of the drapery— than in any other picture of his that is known to us. Next to it in date are the angel in Verrocchio's "Baptism," and the

---

[8] Francesco Albertini, *Memoriale* (Firenze, 1510): ". . . . in Sancto Salvi tavole bellissime, et uno angelo di Leonardo Vinci."

"Annunciation" in the Uffizi. The "Annunciation" is a composite work, the Angel Annunciant, and, in fact, the design of the picture being by Leonardo, whilst the figure of the Virgin and her reading-desk were executed, I believe, by his fellow-student, Domenico Ghirlandajo.

Of the same period is the portrait of Ginevra dei Benci, which is in the Liechtenstein Gallery. The bush of juniper in the background of the picture, and a branch of the same plant painted on the reverse side of the panel, confirm the view that this work is a portrait of a lady named Ginevra, and that it is the picture referred to by the Anonimo Gaddiano in a passage in which he states that "Leonardo drew from life, in Florence, Ginevra d'Amerigo Benci."[9]

Verrocchio, when still a young man, had been appointed official artist of the Medici. In the year 1464, he received the commission for the simple tombstone of Cosimo de' Medici, Pater Patriae. It was to be placed at the foot of the High Altar in San Lorenzo.[10] After the death of Donato de' Medici, Bishop of Pistoia, in 1474, he received a commission, from the prelate's executors, to paint a great altarpiece for the chapel of the bishop in the Cathedral of Pistoia.[11] It was expressly stipulated, in the original agreement, that Verrocchio was to furnish the executors with his designs for the *ancona*, and that he was to be responsible for its execution.[12] This altarpiece was "almost finished" in the year 1478, or in 1479, and, perhaps, even at an earlier date. As Leonardo was Verrocchio's chief assistant, and the head of the department of painting in his workshop at the time that it was being made, he must have had some share in the work. The only portions of it, however, in which we can clearly detect the hand of the younger artist, are in the vest-

[9] Anonimo Gaddiano, *Il Codice Magliabecchiano*, in the Biblioteca Nazionale, Florence. See L. Beltrami, *op. cit.*, p. 162.

[10] M. Cruttwell, *Verrocchio* (London, 1904), pp. 30, 31, 75–77.

[11] See Appendix I.

[12] In a letter of the Operai del Duomo, dated November, 1485, we are told that the picture, which had been "almost finished" more than six years before, had been put on one side because the bishop's executors had not made the payments that were due. See Appendix I.

ments of San Donato d'Arezzo—one of the two male saints that are represented in the altarpiece—and in two panels of the predella. One of these panels is the "Annunciation" at the Louvre, a painting that was regarded until recently, by all the leading critics of Italian art of the last fifty years, as the finest work of Leonardo's early period.[13] The other is the newly-discovered "San Donato and the Tax Collector," now at Worcester, Massachusetts.

It seems to be certain that the "Madonna with the Vase of Flowers" at Munich belongs to the same period as the "Madonna di Piazza," that is to say that it was painted during the last months of Leonardo's close co-operation with Verrocchio. This picture is in a poor state of preservation and much repainted. Nevertheless, there is enough of the original work left to make it clear that it is from the hand of Leonardo, though one of his least admirable pictures.

In the year 1476, when Leonardo was living in his master's house in Florence, he had to face a serious indictment. With several other young men, some of them members of noble Florentine families, he had to appear before the city magistrates on a charge of sodomy. The case was not dismissed: it was regarded as not proved; and the defendants were required to present themselves again at the court at a later date. On their second appearance, the bench arrived at a similar inconclusive decision.[14] That these charges had some basis appears to be probable when regarded in the light of much that is known to us of Leonardo's later life. His homosexual tendencies are not only manifested in inscriptions on drawings: "his homosexual-

[13] In an article entitled "Leonardo as Verrocchio's Co-worker" (*Art Bulletin*, March, 1930, p. 50), Valentiner states that "the 'Annunciation' of the Louvre is generally regarded as a work by Leonardo." Gronau (*Leonardo da Vinci* [London: Duckworth], p. 70) tells us that this "Annunciation" is "the one early work of the master upon which opinions are agreed, and that it is generally recognized as a painting by Leonardo's own hand." Until quite recently this painting was ascribed by general consent to Leonardo by all the leading authorities on the master—Bode, Morelli, Bayersdorfer, A. Venturi, L. Venturi, Berenson, Seidlitz, Valentiner, Gronau, Thiis, McCurdy, Aldo de Rinaldis, Suida, Bodmer, Kenneth Clark, and Degenhart. Poggi writes: "The attribution to Leonardo proposed by Giovanni Morelli was universally accepted by the more competent critics" (see G. Poggi, *op. cit.*, "Annotazioni alle Tavole," p. ii).

[14] Herbert P. Horne, *The Life of Leonardo da Vinci by Giorgio Vasari* (London, 1903), p. 12.

ity is," in fact, as Kenneth Clark writes, "implicit in a large section of his work." Such a feature of his character would not concern the art critic had it not had a marked effect on Leonardo's art.[15]

The Anonimo Gaddiano tells us that, as a young man, Leonardo attracted the notice of Lorenzo il Magnifico; and that it was arranged that he should work in the Garden of the Medici in the Piazza di San Marco.[16] It seems, however, that he still continued to act as an assistant to Verrocchio until 1478, in which year he began to accept independent commissions. It was, no doubt, owing to the influence of his patron Lorenzo that Leonardo, in January, 1478, was chosen to paint the altarpiece of the Chapel of the Signoria of Florence. This work was never completed.

[15] Kenneth Clark, *Leonardo da Vinci* (Cambridge, England, and New York, 1939), pp. 54, 55.

[16] L. Beltrami, *op. cit.*, p. 161, Doc. 254.

CHAPTER II

LEONARDO'S LIFE
1478-1500

THE year 1478 proved to be a turning-point in the artist's life. Until then, whilst his works had shown much promise, none of them had been of supreme importance.— This is clear from the fact that all the paintings that belong to his first period, that is to say all the works attributed to Leonardo that were painted in or before the year 1478, have, at one time or another, been attributed, by the chief critics of Italian painting, to quite second-rate artists.—Now Leonardo begins to emerge from the tutelage of a dominant personality, and to develop with extraordinary rapidity his own individual style.

In his list of Leonardo drawings, Heinrich Bodmer places amongst those of his early time certain drawings of a mother and her child. These drawings are the "Madonna and Child with a Plate of Fruit" in the Louvre, the "Madonna del Fiore" in the British Museum, and the studies for a "Madonna of the Cat." The first and second of these drawings were preliminary sketches for the picture now at Leningrad, which is known as the Benois "Madonna," the earliest-known work of this period of transition. There is no record of the picture by Leonardo that had for its subject the "Madonna of the Cat."[1] All these drawings, it seems, were made in, or immediately before the year 1478, in which year, as we learn from an inscription on a drawing of his in the Uffizi, Leonardo "began to paint two Madonnas."[2] It is interesting to note that, as soon as Leonardo was free to choose his own subjects, he painted pictures of the Virgin and Child.

[1] Enrico Bodmer, *Disegni di Leonardo* (Florence, 1939), p. 13, Pls. 1, 2, and 3. See Appendix II.

[2] H. Bodmer, *Leonardo: Des Meisters Gemälde und Zeichnungen* ("Klassiker der Kunst" Series [Stuttgart, 1931]), p. 115.

It was in this same year, it seems, that the young artist first met his future patron, Lodovico il Moro, who, in 1478, came to Florence to condole with Lorenzo il Magnifico, after the assassination of Lorenzo's brother Giuliano.[3] In December, 1479, the artist made a drawing of one of the assassins, Bandino Baroncelli, when the murderer's body was displayed to the public, hanging from a window of the Palazzo della Signoria.

This period of rapid progress culminated in the year 1481, when Leonardo began that unfinished masterpiece, the "Adoration of the Magi." He had received a commission from the monks of S. Donato a Scopeto to paint a picture for the High Altar of their church; and he seems to have entered upon his task with great enthusiasm. His fervor had not cooled when he began to paint, in umber and terra verde, the main part of the picture, wherein he represented the Virgin and Child, and the adoring crowd gazing at their long-promised Savior, the Light of the World. Nevertheless, in the following year, in 1482, he left the picture unfinished, and set out for Milan. He also left unfinished the small "St. Jerome" which is now in the Vatican Gallery.

Leonardo, we are told, had been commended to Lodovico il Moro, uncle and guardian of the young Duke of Milan, as a musician and a brilliant performer on a silver lyre. But the draft of a remarkable letter by Leonardo, which is in the *Codice Atlantico*,[4] leads us to conclude that there were more substantial reasons for his summons to Milan. In this letter Leonardo writes, at some length, on his qualifications as a military engineer. He claims to be able to make light bridges and secret tunnels for use in war, as well as artillery of different kinds and large tanks. He also claims that in time of peace he can rival anyone in the construction of canals, and in the arts of architecture, sculpture, and painting.

[3] Archivio di Stato, Milano, Doc. Diplomatici, Dominio Sforzesco: Duca Gian Galeazzo, *Lettera di Filippo Sacramoro, legato Sforzesco a Firenze, in seguito all' uccisione di Giuliano de' Medici.* See L. Beltrami, *Documenti e Memorie riguardanti la Vita e le Opere di Leonardo da Vinci* (Milan: Fratelli Treves, 1919), p. 6.

[4] L. Beltrami, *op. cit.*, pp. 10, 11; J. P. and Irma A. Richter, *The Literary Works of Leonardo da Vinci* (London and New York, 1939), II, 325-27.

But the real purpose of the letter—as is so often the case—is disclosed in one of its concluding paragraphs. Leonardo sought to obtain from the Duke the commission to execute the equestrian statue to the memory of Francesco Sforza, Lodovico's great father. This work had long been planned and was the chief artistic project of the actual ruler of Milan, who, like the bad uncle of so many romances and melodramas, had usurped the rights of his nephew, the nominal head of the state. Leonardo was ambitious to rival and surpass the "Gattamelata" of Donatello, as well as the Colleoni statue that his former master was then engaged upon in Venice.

But there were other reasons that led him to seek employment in Milan. Verrocchio and his followers no longer held the paramount position that they had once occupied in Florence. Lorenzo il Magnifico, himself a poet of no mean order, found in the beautiful recorded dreams of the painter of the "Primavera" and the "Birth of Venus" something that touched him more deeply than did the works of Verrocchio. Leonardo, too, was without doubt influenced by the fact that Milan, after Venice, was the richest state in Italy, and that it had for its ruler a man of great wealth and a generous patron of the arts. It must have come to his knowledge that Lodovico il Moro was ambitious to beautify Milan, and to make his Court a center of Italian culture.

Having left unfinished in Florence at least two commissions for pictures, it seems that Leonardo, on his arrival in Milan, was in immediate need of money. Only this can account for the fact that he agreed to paint, for a miserable remuneration, for the Confraternity of the Immaculate Conception of that city, a "Madonna and Child and Angels," to fit the central part of a large altarpiece, for which an elaborate frame had already been made, at considerable cost, by Giacomo del Maino, one of the wood-carvers of the choir stalls of the Certosa di Pavia. This contract had been obtained for him and for Ambrogio de Predis by Ambrogio's brother, Evangelista Preda, who acted, it appears, as a kind of art agent in Milan. The *ancona*, it was agreed, was to consist of five panels, a large central panel—a

Madonna and Child, with four lateral panels of Angels. It would appear, however, that only two of these four panels of Angels were completed. Leonardo painted the "Madonna and Child," the central part of the work, whilst Ambrogio painted the two other panels. This central panel was the "Virgin of the Rocks," which is now in the Louvre.

The painting was almost finished, and the stipulated payments made. But the artists were by no means satisfied. They complained that they had received a wholly inadequate sum from the Confraternity, a sum which did not cover the expenses incurred in the work. They sought to get possession of the picture, as they knew that they could get a better price for it elsewhere. A legal action was begun which dragged on for more than twenty years. Finally, during the time when the French were in occupation of Milan, in the year 1506, Louis XII, who was an enthusiastic admirer of Leonardo's Madonnas, evidently succeeded in getting possession of the central panel of the altarpiece, the "Virgin of the Rocks." The Confraternity who first commissioned the altarpiece agreed to accept in its place a replica, which is now in the National Gallery in London.

That the new picture was taken in hand immediately, in accordance with the agreement, is probably why Louis's minister, Charles d'Amboise, Seigneur de Chaumont, wrote an urgent letter to the Signory of Florence on May 30, 1506, begging that body to permit Leonardo to return to Milan. Leonardo returned, and designed the replica which the Confraternity had, it seems, agreed to accept. The execution of it, however, was intrusted by the master to one of his Milanese followers, whose identity has not yet been satisfactorily established.

As a matter of fact, there is no existing document that proves that Louis succeeded in acquiring the "Virgin of the Rocks" in 1506 and that the Confraternity accepted a replica in its place. This hypothesis of Giovanni Poggi,[5] however, is the one that best accords with the known facts. The "Virgin of the Rocks" belongs in style to Leonardo's second Florentine period, the

[5] G. Poggi, *Leonardo da Vinci, La Vita di Giorgio Vasari, Nuovamente Commentata e Illustrata,* etc. (Florence, 1919), pp. vi–xiv. See Appendix III.

brief period that began in 1478, whilst the National Gallery altarpiece is obviously considerably later in date. Moreover, Poggi's hypothesis receives confirmation from a letter written by Chaumont to the Signoria of Florence on August 15, 1507.[6] In this letter, Chaumont states that it was with the greatest difficulty that permission had been obtained for Leonardo da Vinci, painter to the most Christian King, to pay a visit to Florence, as he had bound himself to make a picture for his royal employer. This picture, it seems, the king was very anxious to see finished at an early date.

But to return to the events of 1482, in which year Leonardo arrived in Milan. At that time, he was, as we have seen, in need of money. He was soon relieved of anxiety on this score; as he received from Lodovico the important commission that he had coveted, and was given the very liberal annual salary of two thousand ducats. He was chosen to make "The Horse," as it was called, the equestrian statue of Lodovico's father—a task which occupied him, at intervals, for sixteen years, and which he finally left unfinished.

During these years in Milan Leonardo undoubtedly painted many pictures, wholly or in part, as Bandello testifies; but he also devoted much time to other pursuits. As a civil engineer, he concerned himself with plans for canalization. As a military engineer, he designed engines of war. As an architect, he studied the construction of domes—the domes of churches—a subject that then occupied the attention of his friend Bramante. Moreover, in course of time, he became a kind of factotum to the Court of Milan. In the years that followed Lodovico's marriage, he arranged masques and pageants at the bidding of the young Duchess; and, as her architect, he planned a pavilion for her garden at Vigevano—the favorite residence of Lodovico and Beatrice—and arranged a hot-water installation for her bathroom.[7]

But he did not forget his primary vocation. In the year 1492,

[6] L. Beltrami, *op. cit.*, p. 120.

[7] *Codice Atlantico*, fol. 104r.b; J. P. and I. A. Richter, *op. cit.*, II, 180.

and again in the year 1494, Leonardo passed some months at Vigevano; and it was, no doubt, during his second long visit to the castle, that he painted the Duke and Duchess and also received commissions for portraits of other members of the Court. Some of these portraits he painted himself; others he intrusted to pupils, supervising their work, and sometimes adding finishing touches to it. Amongst the portraits of this time that are not entirely by the master's own hand, I would now place "La Belle Ferronière," which must be regarded as, for the most part, a work of his best Milanese assistant, Giovanni Antonio Boltraffio. Another portrait of this type, though not equal to it in quality, is the "Portrait of a Lady as Venus," by Marco d'Oggiono, which is in the Lederer Collection. At a somewhat later date, Leonardo was commissioned to paint Lodovico's mistress, Lucrezia Crivelli. This portrait cannot now be identified.

It was during this first period of his residence in Milan, in July, 1490, that Leonardo took into his employ the boy Salai, who was then but ten years old. "He was," says Vasari, "most comely in grace and beauty, having fine locks, abundant and curly, in which Leonardo much delighted." This description of Salai is borne out by the evidence of the master's drawings. Unfortunately for Leonardo, the boy, though good to look at, had a bad character. He was a habitual pilferer and liar, his master complains. He was also greedy and gluttonous, and wholly unreliable. Leonardo records the boy's misdoings, but he does not dismiss him from his service. In fact Salai continued to be Leonardo's personal servant until his master's death.[8]

We conclude, from the evidence of some of Leonardo's drawings at Windsor,[9] and from the background of the "Monna Lisa," that, during his first period in Milan, he visited the High Alps. "Indubbiamente," writes Malaguzzi-Valeri, "il paesaggio di *Monna Lisa* è ispirato dal vero."[10] But I cannot

[8] Salai's name was Gian Giacomo de' Caporotti detto "Salai" (see E. Moeller, "Salai und Leonardo da Vinci," *Jahrbuch der Kunsthistorischen Sammlungen in Wien*, N.F., II [1928], 139-61; also L. Beltrami, *Arch. Stor. Lombardo* [1916]).

[9] Nos. 12.409, 12.408, 12.407, 12.399. See Pls. IV, V, and VI.

[10] F. Malaguzzi-Valeri, *La Corte di Ludovico il Moro* (Milan, 1915), II, 579, 580.

agree with the writer when he proceeds to surmise that the artist drew his inspiration from the low hills and the rounded rocks of the Adda Valley. A tireless pilgrim of science, continually urged forward by an insatiable thirst for knowledge, a romantic artist, with a passion for nature's most horrific aspects, Leonardo, when visiting Chiavenna and Tirano, would not have missed the opportunity of enjoying the stark beauty of the Val Bregaglia, and the sublime grandeur of the High Alps as seen from the near-by Engadine Valley. The drawing, a "Storm in the Alps," which is at Windsor,[11] was without doubt drawn from nature, from some spot above Zuoz in the Upper Engadine. This drawing in red chalk is a little later in date than the drawings for the "Last Supper," that is to say it was made in the last few years of Leonardo's residence in Milan.

Undoubtedly, many important drawings of this period have not come down to us. One of these lost drawings must, I think, have been a sketch of the Upper Engadine Valley as seen from Muottas Murail. For it was this view, I believe, that Leonardo had in mind when he painted the background of the "Monna Lisa." As was the case with Leonardo's drawings for his early representations of the Madonna, the drawing must have been more naturalistic than the painting. It is not possible to decide precisely on what date Leonardo was in the Valtellina; but it is clear from the evidence of his writings,[12] and his drawings, that he did visit that valley and the neighboring valleys, and that, as Lodovico's engineer, he was sent to the Milanese border fortresses of Chiavenna and Tirano, perhaps accompanied by Ambrogio Ferrari, the Duke's Commissario-Generale for fortifications.[13] Knowing well Chiavenna itself and the surrounding country, I am convinced that one of the drawings at Windsor,[14]

[11] No. 12.409, Pl. IV.

[12] In the *Codice Atlantico* (fol. 214a) is a description of the Valtellina. On the recto side of it occurs the name of Ambrogio Ferrari.

[13] Mario Cermanati, "Leonardo in Valtellina," *Per il Centenario della Morte di Leonardo da Vinci* (Roma: Istituto di Studi Vinciani, 1919), p. 210.

[14] H. Bodmer, *Leonardo*, p. 263. It is unfortunate that this drawing (No. 12.399), and some other drawings, are not well reproduced in Sir Kenneth Clark's indispensable work on the drawings of

represents that fortified town, and that it was made while Leonardo was in the service of the Duke of Milan.

It seems to be probable that, as Lodovico's military engineer, Leonardo made more than one visit to Chiavenna and Tirano in the Valtellina; and it is more than likely that he was in that valley for a short time in 1496. For in the middle of July in that year, the Duke, with a great train of ambassadors and high dignitaries of the Church, of military officers and engineers, as well as of artists and men of letters, set out to pay a brief visit to the Emperor Maximilian and his niece, the Empress, at Mals. Both going and returning, he passed through the Valtellina; and on his way home he broke his journey at Chiavenna. It seems reasonable to conclude that Leonardo was in the Duke's suite.

Altogether too much importance has been given, by some writers, to the contents of a letter[15] that Calco, the Duke's secretary, wrote on June 8, 1496, to the Archbishop of Milan, who was then visiting Venice. In this letter, Calco asked the prelate to try to obtain the services of Perugino for the decoration of the Camerini in the Castello Sforzesco, as a certain artist who was employed on this job had absented himself because of some scandal. Several artists were employed at the Castello; and it is by no means certain that Leonardo was the artist referred to in this document, or that he took any active part in the work there before the spring of 1498. In any case, we know, on the testimony of Matteo Bandello,[16] who was himself a friar of the convent of Santa Maria delle Grazie and the nephew of its Prior, that, for some time before January, 1497, Leonardo had been on good terms with Lodovico, receiving from him a

---

Leonardo da Vinci at Windsor (*A Catalogue of the Drawings of Leonardo da Vinci in the Collection of His Majesty the King at Windsor Castle* [Cambridge University Press, 1935]). It is interesting to note that in this drawing we see a large house in ruins. Chiavenna had been sacked and burned in 1486. See Pl. VI.

15 L. Beltrami, *op. cit.*, p. 40, No. 70.

16 An account of Bandello is given in the Introduction to my edition of Geoffrey Fenton's translation of some of Bandello's *Novelle;* see Sir Geoffrey Fenton, *Certaine Tragicall Discourses,* with an Introduction by R. Langton Douglas ("Tudor Translations" Series [London: Nutt, 1898]). See Appendix IV.

most liberal salary and many gifts. Even if Leonardo had been temporarily involved in some scandal, the despot of Milan would not have allowed that to prevent him from making use of his military engineer, had he made up his mind to do so.[17] A tyrant of the Renaissance soon forgave the peccadilloes and tantrums of an artist, more especially when he found that he was unable to replace him. Moreover, Lodovico had, we know, recently sent to the Emperor a picture by Leonardo, "which was said, by those able to judge it, to be one of the most beautiful and rare works that have been seen in painting."[18] It is but natural that Maximilian should have wished to see the great master. It is probable, therefore, that Leonardo accompanied the Duke, on the occasion of Lodovico's visit to Bormio and Mals,[19] and that, on his homeward journey, he went to the Engadine. In any case, it is certain, from the evidence of Leonardo's drawings and the landscape background of the "Monna Lisa," that, in some summer during his last four years in Milan, he visited that high Alpine valley.

The hypothesis that certain carefully executed drawings at Windsor,[20] in which can be traced, in their backgrounds, dim outlines of high, acuminate peaks,[21] are representations of scenery in the lower Arno Valley, can scarcely be taken seriously by those who know well that valley. The argument that, because in one or two of these drawings we find representations of canals and rivers, they must therefore belong to the first six years of the sixteenth century—when Leonardo was planning the canalization of the Arno—does not help us at all to fix their dates. We know well that the artist was interested in such schemes throughout the whole of his adult life, and never

---

[17] The theory of Müller-Walde and Moeller that there was a long period of dissension at this time between Leonardo and Lodovico is quite untenable today (see G. Calvi, *I Manoscritti di Leonardo da Vinci, dal punto di vista Cronologico, Storico e Biografico* [Bologna: Zanichelli, 1925], pp. 160 and 161).

[18] Anonimo Gaddiano, *Il Codice Magliabecchiano*, ed. Carl Frey (Berlin, 1892), XVII, 17; see L. Beltrami, *op. cit.*, p. 162.

[19] M. Cermanati, *op. cit.*, pp. 232, 234; J. P. and I. A. Richter, *op. cit.*, II, 190.

[20] Nos. 12.406, 12.405, 12.408, 12.399, and 12.398.

[21] H. Bodmer, *Leonardo*, pp. 405, 263, 264, and Enrico Bodmer, *Disegni di Leonardo*, p. 26 and Pls. 75*a* and 75*b*.

more than in his first Milanese period. It seems clear that these drawings of Alpine scenery were made, as Heinrich Bodmer concludes, in the years 1496-99 or, to be more precise, between the middle of July, 1496, and the end of August, 1499; and that they represent places visited by this passionate lover of those high mountains that are the storehouses of tempests.

It was in the latter part of the year 1496 that Leonardo began to paint, at Lodovico's order, his great work, the "Last Supper," on a wall of the Refectory of the Dominican Convent of Santa Maria delle Grazie. In the execution of this work, the artist was certainly not dilatory. But, characteristically, he failed to acquaint himself with the state of the wall on which his picture was to be painted, and, rejecting the old and tried technical process of *buon fresco*, he chose to paint the "Last Supper" in *tempera forte*.[22] Twenty years later, it had begun to crumble and perish;[23] and when Lomazzo saw it on some date before 1584, the painting was entirely ruined.

The "Last Supper" was almost finished at the end of 1497. It was then that the artist at last began to decorate the Camerini, two rooms in the Castello Sforzesco, the Sala delle Asse, and the Saletta Negra, which he had been commissioned to decorate more than two years before. Leonardo's frescoes in the Saletta Negra have entirely disappeared; and the faint remaining traces of those decorations that survive in the Sala delle Asse have been entirely overpainted.

It was after the untimely death of his Duchess, at the beginning of the year 1497, that Lodovico's difficulties began to accumulate. As a consequence, Leonardo's regular salary was left unpaid; and there was little money to devote to artistic projects. But the strained relations that occasionally existed between the artist and Lodovico have been exaggerated and misdated. Leonardo had acquired an unfortunate habit of grumbling on paper—in drafts of letters[24] and, sometimes, in brief,

[22] F. Malaguzzi-Valeri, *op. cit.*, II, 530. Pl. XLV.

[23] L. Beltrami, *op. cit.*, pp. 149, 150. The passage is taken from the *Itinerario* of Antonio de Beatis.

[24] *Codice Atlantico*, fols. 315v and 335. These extracts from drafts of letters belong without doubt to the year 1498.

penned ejaculations of annoyance. These complaints and protests have been regarded too seriously by some of his biographers.

In the year 1497 he began to have some solid grounds for
grumbling. He naturally objected when the stipend that was
due to him from his chief employer was not regularly paid. He
shrank, too, from occupying himself with unremunerative jobs
—such as that in the Camerini—at a time when he was engaged
in two of the most important commissions ever intrusted to
him. But he was not unreasonable; and the Duke and Leonardo
had now a new bond of sympathy in their common aversion to
Savonarola, who was then at the height of his power. Lodovico
actually went so far as to hire assassins to kill the friar. And,
when that plot failed, he caused spurious letters purporting to
have been written by Savonarola to be circulated amongst
the princes of neighboring states, with the object of defeating
the Dominican's political plans. Lodovico did not forget his
debt to Leonardo. In fact, one of his last acts, in the months
preceding his flight from Milan, was to present Leonardo with
a vineyard outside the Porta Vercellina.[25]

Some writers have conjectured that the chief reason why
Leonardo did not complete the equestrian statue of Francesco
Sforza was that funds were not forthcoming for the work, and
that after the year 1494, when Lodovico had sent the bronze
collected for "The Horse" to Ercole d'Este to be made into
cannon, the project for casting it was not revived. We know,
however, on the testimony of an eyewitness, Matteo Bandello,[26] that, at some time in the summer of 1496, Leonardo was
actually at work on "The Horse." It is certain, in fact, that the
project of casting it in bronze had been revived. Had Leonardo,
however, persisted in his attempt to cast the statue, it can-

[25] L. Beltrami, *op. cit.*, pp. 58, 59. In the Deed of Gift, Lodovico speaks of Leonardo in the
highest terms.

[26] M. Bandello, *Novelle* (Lucca, 1554), pp. 363, 364. Kenneth Clark says that we have no
evidence that Lodovico seriously revived the idea of completing "The Horse" after 1494. He for-
gets this statement of Bandello, who was personally acquainted with Leonardo. He also ignores
the testimony of Sabba da Castiglione that the model of "The Horse" occupied Leonardo "for
sixteen consecutive years" (Kenneth Clark, *Catalogue of the Drawings . . . . at Windsor Castle*, I,
XLII). See Appendix IV.

not be doubted that the experiment would have resulted in failure and humiliation.

There is, in fact, abundant evidence of his inability to complete this commission on which he had been engaged for sixteen years. Even Lodovico, his loyal patron, had come to the conclusion, as early as the year 1489, that his artist was unable to cast "The Horse." For, in that year, he caused a letter to be written to Lorenzo de' Medici asking him to send to Milan one or two artists who could cast a bronze statue.[27] We know, too, on the testimony of a witness of the incident, Giovanni da Gavina, that, after Leonardo's return to Florence, Michelangelo taunted him to his face with his inability to cast his model.[28] The older master, we are told, made no reply, but blushed with shame. Leonardo must, in fact, have been relieved when, at last, he had some excuse for relinquishing a hopeless task.

The true reason why "The Horse" was not finished is quite clear. It was due to the same cause that brought about Leonardo's failure to complete satisfactorily all of his major undertakings. As was the case with his great mural paintings, the "Last Supper" and the "Battle of Anghiari," he began with much ardor the task that he had undertaken before he had gained sufficient practical knowledge of his medium of expression. Interested as he was in too many subjects, he had not the time and the patience to acquire subsequently the necessary technical information and skill—as Michelangelo set himself to do, a few years later, after the failure of his first attempt to paint in fresco on the ceiling of the Sistine Chapel.

Louis XII, on his accession to the throne of France, had announced his intention of making good his claim to the Duchy of Milan; and, in alliance with the Venetians, he soon set about the task. In August, 1499, his troups invaded the Milanese territory; and, on October 6, the French king made a triumphal entry into Milan. He remained there but one month, and,

---

[27] Archivio di Stato, Florence, Arch. Mediceo, avanti il Principato, Filza n. 159. This letter is printed by L. Beltrami, *op. cit.*, p. 25. It does not seem that anything resulted from this appeal, for in 1490 Leonardo returned to his work on the statue.

[28] Anonimo Gaddiano, *op. cit.*, p. 115.

during that time, was, of course, much occupied with plans for consolidating his conquests. The foreign soldiers, because of their rapacity and arrogance, made themselves hated by the people of Milan. "The French are a dirty people," wrote one of their allies. "In the Castello Sforzesco, there is nothing but foulness and filth." The young Baldassare Castiglione, in a letter to his mother, confirms this testimony of the Venetian writer.

Leonardo was not in the city when Louis entered Milan; nor was he present when the French king visited the convent of Santa Maria delle Grazie. On his return to Milan, the artist was soon occupied with preparations for leaving the city that had been his home for nearly eighteen years. There is no reason to suppose that, at this time, Louis gave any commission to his arch-enemy's military engineer. Had Leonardo found, at once, a new patron as powerful and exalted as the King of France and had he been intrusted by that patron with some important task, would he have left Milan, as he did a few weeks later, without showing any intention of returning? He approached, it is true, one of the French generals, the Count de Ligny, a former friend of Lodovico il Moro; but this he did with the object of getting back the vineyard that the Duke had recently given him.

Padre Sebastiano Resta, a wholly unreliable writer,[29] whose extraordinary credulity and inaccuracy have been justly castigated by Lanzi and Tiraboschi, declared, nearly two centuries later, that Leonardo was commissioned by Louis XII to execute a picture of the "Virgin and Child and St. Anne," and that the artist had made in Milan, at this time, the cartoon which is now in London. He produced no evidence in support of these statements; and the value of his testimony, on any question relating to Leonardo, may be judged by the fact that, in the brief letter in which he makes this statement, he also asserts that Leonardo died in 1542 and that the artist made, *in Milan*, in the year 1500, a second cartoon of the "Madonna and St. Anne."[30]

[29] See Appendix V.

[30] Gio. Bottari and Stefano Ticozzi, *Raccolta di Lettere sulla Pittura*, etc. (Milan: Silvestri, 1822), III, 481.

For stylistic reasons, it is impossible to accept those theories regarding the date of the cartoon in London that are based on Resta's unsupported statement, made, as we have said, two hundred years after its execution. The stylistic motives of this cartoon, as well as its technical qualities, are fatal to the hypothesis that it can have been executed before 1500. In its whole conception, it is a work of the sixteenth century, and belongs to that period of the Florentine Renaissance in which Leonardo played so significant a part.[31]

On arriving in Florence in the spring of 1500, there began for Leonardo, as we shall presently see, a new period of accelerated development. This development was due, in some measure, to the influence of Michelangelo. But it was also a consequence of the artist's contact with the cultural atmosphere of his own home town, the Metropolis of the Renaissance, to which he had returned after so long an absence. Both in its broad masterly treatment of line and in its more subtle chiaroscuro it shows a great advance on the "Last Supper."[32]

Some recent writers on Leonardo imagine that the fact that Milanese artists subsequently painted pictures largely based on the first cartoon favors the view that this cartoon was made in Milan. It does nothing of the kind. Such an assumption is based upon a complete misapprehension of the history of Leonardo's cartoons. *Leonardo kept his cartoons;* and they were used, sometimes at long intervals of time, by his pupils and followers. The only one of them that we know that he relinquished was one of the two portrait-cartoons of Isabella d'Este, which he gave to that lady. He may, too, have given his uncle a cartoon that he made of Adam and Eve.[33] The first cartoon of the "Virgin and Child and St. Anne" and other cartoons of the artist were made use of by his pupils, after he returned to Milan in the year 1506.

[31] For a reproduction of the Burlington House cartoon, see the Frontispiece of this volume.

[32] It was not until the manuscript of this book had gone to the press that I read Dr. Heinrich Bodmer's note on the cartoon in London. This note gives strong confirmation to the views that I have expressed on its date (see H. Bodmer, *Leonardo*, p. 408).

[33] G. Poggi, *op. cit.*, p. 7.

Leonardo's long period of residence in Milan had been singularly unfruitful. "The Horse" to which he had devoted so much time and thought had not been cast in bronze; and the model of it was soon to be destroyed. His first great experiment in mural painting, the "Last Supper," began to perish before the death of its creator. He did execute, however, certain portraits which still exist, as well as others which have been lost, or which cannot be identified; and he had succeeded in creating one work of transcendent beauty, the "Virgin of the Rocks."

Whilst at Mantua, Leonardo made two cartoons for a portrait of Isabella d'Este, one of which he took with him to Venice, where it was seen by the lutanist, Gusnasco da Pavia. Gusnasco wrote to Isabella, telling her that it was "very well done, and in fact, could not be better." Leonardo had promised the Marchioness that he would make a painting from the cartoon; but this promise was not fulfilled, despite the lady's repeated appeals. It seems probable that, notwithstanding certain imperfections, the cartoon of the Louvre is that which Leonardo kept in his own possession. He soon forgot, however, about the portrait, and became absorbed once more in one of his favorite avocations, that of military engineer. He agreed to advise the Venetians how best to defend themselves against a threatened Turkish invasion, and it was with this object that he paid a brief visit to Friuli, before setting out for Florence.

CHAPTER III

LEONARDO'S LIFE
1500-1519

IN THE month of April, in the year 1500, Leonardo returned to Florence, after nearly twenty years of absence. He found himself once again, as we have said, in the inspiring atmosphere of that city. The effect was instantaneous. The master, as we shall see, produced at once his loveliest creation—the cartoon of the "Madonna and Child and St. Anne," which is in the Diploma Gallery of the Royal Academy in London; and, in the course of the next six years, he did more fine work than he had accomplished in all his long period of residence in Milan.

The fame of Leonardo's "Last Supper" had reached Florence; and, on his arrival there, the Servi di Maria commissioned him to paint an altarpiece for their church, the Santissima Annunziata. That this Order should have given him his first commission was what might have been anticipated; for Leonardo, since his childhood, had been associated with the Annunziata. His father, who was still alive, was Procurator of the Monastery;[1] and Leonardo himself, as a young man, must have frequently visited it. It cannot be doubted, too, that the Servants of Mary, who had been, from their foundation, devoted to the cult of the Divine Mother, themselves chose the subject of the altarpiece. Vasari's statement that Filippino Lippi magnanimously agreed to relinquish a commission that he had received from the monks in order that the picture might be painted by Leonardo is probably without foundation. For not only had Filippino's picture an entirely different subject, it was also, we have reason to believe, far larger in size.[2]

[1] Archivio di Stato, Florence, Conventi soppressi: SS. Annunziata in Firenze, May, 1470 (see Luca Beltrami, *Documenti e Memorie riguardanti la Vita e le Opere di Leonardo da Vinci* [Milan: Fratelli Treves, 1919], p. 3).

[2] Aldo de Rinaldis, *Storia dell'Opera Pittorica di Leonardo da Vinci* (Bologna: Zanichelli, 1926), pp. 233, 234.

The reasons that prompted the Servites in their choice of a subject for their altarpiece seem to have escaped the notice of writers on Leonardo, though they are obvious enough to those who are acquainted with the developments of Catholic theology and hagiography in the latter half of the fifteenth century. During that period, the religious orders that were devoted to the cult of Mary had stressed the importance of the doctrine of the Immaculate Conception. The acceptance of this dogma led, in the course of time, to the adoption of the thesis that the Virgin's mother was a woman of great sanctity. The old legends that told that St. Anne had three husbands and three daughters became more and more discredited. This movement in Catholic theology reached its culminating point in 1494, on the publication of a book in praise of St. Anne, by a famous German scholar, Johannes Trithemius, Abbot of Sponheim.[3] St. Anne, wrote the author, was chosen by God for her appointed service before the foundation of the world. She conceived "without the action of man," and was as pure as her daughter. "Why then," Trithemius asks, "do we not honour the mother as we honour the daughter?"

Thirty years later this new cult provoked the protests of Luther; and, in a subsequent age, the Church itself condemned the doctrine that St. Anne was a virgin. But in the years that followed the publication of Trithemius' book, those orders that were devoted to Mary, such as the Confréries de la Conception and the Servites of Mary, not only employed painters to set before the unlearned the doctrine of the Immaculate Conception, they also engaged artists to represent the part that St. Anne played in the divine scheme of Redemption. It was precisely at this time that Leonardo was commissioned to paint a picture of the "Virgin and Child and St. Anne," by the parent-house of that great Catholic order, the Servites of Mary.

Leonardo drew two cartoons for the altarpiece. The first he must have made soon after his arrival in Florence in the month of April in the year 1500.[4] This first cartoon, it seems, did not

---

[3] J. Trithemius, *De Laudibus sanctissimae Matris Annae tractatus* (Mainz, 1494).

[4] This, I find, is also the opinion of Dr. Bodmer (see above, p. 23, n. 22).

satisfy his patrons. The reason for this is clear. The cartoon now in London is a work of great beauty; but, as was natural in the case of Leonardo, the design was not sufficiently didactic in character for the theologians of the Annunziata. It was, in fact, just a beautiful presentation of happy family life. "No one," writes Pater, "ever ruled over his subject more entirely than Leonardo, or bent it more dexterously to purely artistic ends." The Servites, however, wished their altarpiece to teach the people certain profound doctrines, to explain to the unlearned—in so far as it can be explained to mortal minds—the mystery of the Incarnation. Leonardo, we conclude, was asked to prepare a second cartoon, more in accordance with their wishes. In order to help him to devote himself to the task, they gave him and all his assistants a lodging in their house. But it was a long time before Leonardo produced the second cartoon, the cartoon that they wanted. In fact, it was not finished at the beginning of April, 1501. "His life," writes Isabella d'Este's correspondent in Florence, Fra Pietro da Novellara, "is extremely variable and undetermined, so that he seems to live from day to day."[5] He had certainly strong temptation to give way to his accustomed fickleness. His friend Luca Pacioli, the great mathematician, had returned to Florence with him, and Leonardo was deeply interested in geometrical problems. But, nevertheless, moved by the Servites' appeals,[6] he produced, at last, a second cartoon that fully met their requirements.

This second cartoon no longer exists, but we know that it was replete with spiritual significance, for we have a detailed report of it by a contemporary theologian. Fra Pietro da Novellara, who was the Vicar General of the Carmelites, describes it as follows: The cartoon "represents Christ as a baby of about one year old, who, leaving the arms of his Mother, takes hold of a lamb, and appears as though he were about to hug it. The Mother, half rising from the lap of St. Anne, seizes the Child, in order to take it away from the lamb—the symbol of sacrifice, which

[5] Archivio di Stato, Mantua, Letter of April 3, 1501, written from Florence (see L. Beltrami, *op. cit.*, pp. 65, 66).

[6] G. Vasari, *Le Vite*, ed. G. Milanesi (Florence: Sansoni, 1878–85), IV, 38.

represents the Passion. St. Anne, rising a little from her seat, appears to wish to hold the Child, so that he shall not be separated from the lamb." The friar proceeds to explain that St. Anne, in this cartoon, "is figurative of the Church, which does not desire that the Passion of Christ should be prevented," knowing that by Christ's sacrifice mankind would be saved. This description shows us clearly why the second cartoon was preferred to the first by the Servants of Mary. It contained far more definite religious teaching than did the lovely record of a vision that is now in London.

The second cartoon, when it was finished, had, Vasari tells us, a great popular success. "It caused not only artists to marvel. For men and women, young and old, continued for two days to flock to the room where it was, as though they were going to some solemn festival, in order that they might behold the wonderful work of Leonardo."

The first cartoon, it seems, was put away in Leonardo's cherished collection of cartoons, and was taken to Milan when the artist returned there in the year 1506. There, it was copied by Luini; and Melzi reproduced the figure of the Blessed Virgin, when he designed his "Vertumnus and Pomona," which is now in Berlin. At Berlin, too, is a tame picture by Brescianino, which is based on the lost second cartoon, or on a copy of it.[7]

Fra Pietro da Novellara, on his first visit to Leonardo— which was on or before April 3, 1501—was shown only one work of the artist, the second cartoon of the "Virgin and Child and St. Anne." He tells us that it was not quite finished. It may, indeed, have been on Leonardo's easel when the friar called on him; for we know that the Servites were impatient to get this cartoon, for which they had waited so long. Fra Pietro jumped to the conclusion that this was the only work that Leonardo had done since his arrival in Milan. This, we know, was not the case; and Fra Pietro himself corrected the mistake, in a second letter that he wrote to the Marchioness on the following day.

[7] W. Suida, *Leonardo und sein Kreis* (Munich, 1929), p. 131, Pl. 131. Through a typographical error, the two plates on p. 131 have wrong titles. The titles of the two pictures reproduced on this page have been exchanged.

For, in it, he proceeds to describe another picture that Leonardo had recently made, a small picture of the Madonna, which he had painted for Robertet, "a favourite of the King of France." This picture was the "Madonna with the Yarn-Winder," a work that no longer exists. Several copies of it, made by Leonardo's pupils and followers, have, however, survived. Of all these copies, only one closely resembles the original as it is described by Fra Pietro. This version is by Luini, and is in the collection of Godfrey Locker-Lampson.[8] In it alone do we see the Child, "with his foot in the basket of spindles, gazing attentively at the winder which has the form of a Cross," and "holding it tight, as though he did not wish to give it up to his Mother."[9]

There was another picture that Leonardo had agreed to paint soon after his arrival in Florence. He accepted a commission from Francesco del Giocondo to make a portrait of his young wife, who had recently lost her child. As he had done but a little time before, in the case of the projected portrait of Isabella d'Este, Leonardo, in accordance with his usual practice, made a cartoon for this portrait of "Monna Lisa." He put it on one side, however, when he became absorbed in mathematical problems; and he did not begin to paint the picture itself until after his return from Romagna in 1503.

It was in the summer of 1502 that he left Florence. Abandoning both the commissions that he had undertaken and his mathematical studies, he acted as military engineer to Caesar Borgia, when the Duke was engaged in his bloody campaign in the Romagna. It is true that several other artists of the Renaissance also followed for a time the profession of military engineering. But, as a humanitarian, whose views on the taking of life were almost akin to those of a Jain, Leonardo was guilty of inconsistency, when, more than once, he actually sought to place his remarkable gifts at the disposal of some cruel aggres-

---

[8] R. Langton Douglas, *A Few Italian Pictures Collected by Godfrey Locker-Lampson* (London: Chiswick Press, 1934), p. 30, Pl. XII. There are other good versions of the "Madonna with the Yarn-Winder" in the collections of Prince Rupprecht of Bavaria, the Duke of Buccleuch, and Mr. Robert W. Reford of Montreal; but they differ considerably from the original work.

[9] Archivio di Stato, Mantua, *Lettera a Isabella d'Este, da Firenze, 4 Aprile 1501* (see L. Beltrami, *op. cit.*, pp. 66, 67).

sor. He took part in the attack on Urbino in June of that year; and it was then that he made the acquaintance of Machiavelli. In August, he received a patent from the Duke. In this document, he is described by Caesar Borgia as "nostro Prestantissimo et Dilectissimo Familiare Architecto et Ingengero Generale, Leonardo Vinci."[10] Leonardo continued to accompany his new employer for some months. At the end of that time, however, he had an unpleasant shock: His friend Vitellozzo Vitelli, one of Caesar's captains, was strangled by his master's orders. At the beginning of March, 1503, Leonardo was back in Florence.

It must have been soon after his return that he set to work on the portrait of La Gioconda, at which he labored, Vasari tells us, for four years. The picture was certainly completed before 1506 and perhaps before 1505, as the young Raphael imitated the pose of Monna Lisa in his portrait of Maddalena Doni.

In 1503, with the assistance of his new friend Machiavelli, Leonardo obtained from the Signoria of Florence a commission to make a large fresco for the Sala di Gran Consiglio in the Palazzo della Signoria.[11] In the following year, Michelangelo was called upon to paint a fresco on the opposite wall of this great apartment. Neither of the events chosen for representation was of any historical importance. Leonardo took for his subject the "Battle of Anghiari," a subject which had for its central theme the "Fight for the Standard," because he wished to paint horses and the fury of battle, "the bestial frenzy of war." Michelangelo selected for his subject an episode in the "Battle of Cascina," when a contingent of Pisan soldiers was surprised while bathing, because he liked to paint nude figures.

The two cartoons were indeed made, but neither fresco was ever finished. Leonardo, very characteristically, confected the plaster for it from a recipe of Pliny, which he did not wholly understand. The mixture did not set. The artist succeeded in putting on the wall only one small part of his picture.

In May, 1506, he was invited by Charles d'Amboise, Seigneur

[10] L. Beltrami, *op. cit.*, p. 72, Doc. 117.

[11] L. Beltrami, *op. cit.*, pp. 87–89, Doc. 140.

de Chaumont, to go to Milan, to do some work for the French King, Louis XII.[12] The Signoria reluctantly granted Leonardo three months' leave of absence. Subsequently, Louis asked thrice for an extension of this leave, and thrice it was granted; though in October the public-spirited Gonfaloniere of the Republic, Piero Soderini, in a minute addressed to the Signoria, complained that Leonardo "had not behaved properly to the Republic, because he had received a considerable sum of money from the Government, and had only made a small beginning of the great work that he had engaged to do."[13]

The rulers of Florence had other reasons for being annoyed with Leonardo. Using his undoubted powers of persuasion, Leonardo had prevailed upon the Government to adopt a specious scheme for depriving Pisa of the Arno by altering the course of the stream. He had also planned to make the river navigable up to Florence. The scheme proved to be wholly impracticable and was soon abandoned.

The reason for Leonardo's summons to Milan is explained in a letter written in the following January to the Government of Florence, by Pandolfini, the representative of the Republic at the Court of Milan. Describing an interview with Louis, Pandolfini states that he asked the sovereign what kind of work it was that he desired of Leonardo. "Certain little Madonnas," the king replied. Louis had recently seen a small "Virgin and Child" that had been sent to Milan.—In all probability, it was the "Madonna with the Yarn-Winder."—And he wanted from the artist other paintings of the Virgin and Child. He also wished Leonardo to paint his portrait.[14] It seems likely that it was at this time, when the law-suit regarding the "Virgin of the Rocks" was in process of settlement, that the French King succeeded in purchasing that picture, after promising the Confraternity that had given the commission for the painting that Leonardo would supply a replica of it for their church. The execution of the altarpiece that the

[12] See above, p. 13.

[13] Archivio di Stato, Firenze, Filza 121, October 9, 1506, *Minute di Pier Soderini.*

[14] E. Solmi, *Leonardo* (Florence, 1900), p. 167; L. Beltrami, *op. cit.*, pp. 114, 115.

Confraternity ultimately received, the version of the "Virgin of the Rocks" which is now in the National Gallery in London, is almost entirely the work of a pupil.

It was not until the autumn of 1507 that Leonardo returned to Florence. The object of his journey was to establish his claim to a share in his father's estate. He did not attempt to resume work on the "Battle of Anghiari." He was now the official painter to the Most Christian King, and, in that capacity, was on temporary leave from Milan. In a letter written to Chaumont six months after his departure from that city, he reports: "My litigation with my brothers is almost at an end. I hope to be with you at Easter, and to bring with me two Madonnas."

During this period of residence in Florence, he had lived, so the Anonimo Gaddiano tells us, in the house of Piero di Braccio Martelli. Rustici the sculptor occupied a studio in the same building. According to Vasari, Leonardo assisted Rustici in making the large bronze figures of St. John the Baptist between a Levite and a Pharisee, which the sculptor was then engaged upon modeling for the Baptistery. These figures, I believe, are the only existing sculptures, in bronze or marble, in which we can trace the hand of Leonardo.

On his return to Milan, although Chaumont, his loyal patron, recognized that painting was Leonardo's true vocation, the versatile artist, as was his habit, divided his time amongst a variety of pursuits. Again, as in the days of Lodovico, he acted as the government's architect and engineer; and again he designed sumptuous pageants. He also spent much time in the study of geology and botany, anatomy and embryology.

There are, however, three pictures that have been attributed to Leonardo that were painted about this time. These are the "Virgin and Child and St. Anne" and the "St. John the Baptist" —both of which are now in the Louvre—and the lost picture "Leda," a painting which, when Cassiano del Pozzo saw it in 1625, was in a deplorable state of preservation.

The "Virgin and Child and St. Anne" was designed by Leonardo; but the execution is—as we have already stated— for the most part, the work of an assistant. For this picture, the artist made a cartoon that differed considerably from both of the cartoons for pictures of this subject that he had made in Florence in the years 1500 and 1501.

For the standing "Leda," he also made a cartoon, which was seen by the English traveler Edward Wright, in the year 1720, in the Casnedi collection in Milan.[15] The best of the early copies of the "Leda" made by Leonardo's pupils are in the Borghese Gallery and at Wilton House.

It was near the end of his last period of residence in Milan, in the year 1511, that Leonardo was commissioned to make an equestrian monument for Gian Giacomo Trivulzio, one of the two generals who were placed in command of Milan, after the death of Leonardo's patron, Charles d'Amboise. He again made many drawings of horses, as he had done when at work on the equestrian statue of Francesco Sforza; but Trivulzio's monument, like "The Horse," was never completed. In this case, Leonardo was able to give a good reason for not carrying out his commission. For in the summer of 1512 the French lost Milan, and Leonardo lost his job.

Leonardo had recently made the acquaintance of Francesco Melzi, a young artist of good family, whose ancestral home was at Vaprio, near Milan. It was probably at his villa that Leonardo spent some months, at a time when the city was again full of disorder and violence. Melzi, Vasari tells us, "was, in Leonardo's life-time, a beautiful youth, and much loved by him." "He is to-day," he adds, "a beautiful and gentle old man."

In May, 1513, Giovanni de' Medici, son of Leonardo's old patron, Lorenzo il Magnifico, had been made Pope. Leo X, like his father, was a patron of the arts, as was his brother Giuliano. Four months later, Leonardo, taking with him Melzi, Salai, and two other pupils, set out for Rome, and entered the service of Giuliano. His new employer gave him an apartment in the Belvedere of the Vatican.

Leonardo's life in Rome cannot have been happy. His great rivals Michelangelo and Raphael held strong positions in the

[15] Edward Wright, *Some Observations Made in Travelling through France and Italy, ... in the Years 1720 and 1722* (London, 1730), p. 471.

Eternal City. The old man quarreled too, with his inferiors, his immediate neighbors in the Belvedere, and not without good reason. For a German mechanic, a certain Giovanni degli Specchi—so-called because of his skill as a maker of mirrors —also had an apartment in the Belvedere; and he filled the whole building with his workmen, even intruding into Leonardo's studio, and interrupting his work. More than that, the mirror-maker tried to prejudice the Pope against Leonardo by carrying to the Holy Father slanderous tales regarding the artist's anatomical studies. Nevertheless, in spite of discomfort and annoyances and notwithstanding the fact that he spent much time on a book that he was writing, *De Ludo Geometrico*, and other avocations, his sojourn in Rome was not altogether without tangible results. For he painted three pictures whilst he was there. "He made," says Vasari, "for Messer Baldassare Turini da Pescia, a little picture of Our Lady with the Child in her arms, with infinite diligence and art; but whether through the fault of him who covered the panel with gesso, or because of Leonardo's so many capricious mixtures of grounds and colours, the picture is now in a much ruined state." He also drew, we are told, a "portrait of a boy, which is beautiful and graceful to a marvel." Another picture that, in all probability, was painted in Rome was the portrait of Costanza d'Avalos, the widowed Duchess of Francavilla, heroine of Ischia, who was related to the Colonna. This portrait is referred to in four sonnets by the contemporary poet, Enea Irpino di Parma.[16] Not one of these three paintings has survived. But a picture by Luini, which is in the Proby Collection at Elton Hall, may be a copy of the lost portrait of a boy.[17]

"On the 9th day of January, 1515," Leonardo relates, "Giuliano the Magnificent left Rome to marry a wife in Savoy." In July, Giuliano was taken ill and returned to his native city.

---

[16] L. Beltrami, *op. cit.*, pp. 212 and 213.

[17] The child is represented smiling and holding in his hand a small trick note-case. Similar note-cases were on sale in this country and in England about twenty years ago. It is possible that this kind of note-case or bill-case was one of Leonardo's inventions. The picture was in the collection of Thomas, Earl of Arundel in the first half of the seventeenth century, when it was attributed to Leonardo. Luini, it will be remembered, made copies of other works by Leonardo.

Leonardo, who was attached to his patron's household, probably joined him there. Giuliano died at Fiesole on March 17, 1516.

In a short period of time, Leonardo had lost two of the best patrons that he had ever had. But fate was kind to the aged artist. He passed his last days in peace and comfort, surrounded by admiring friends. For Giuliano had not long been dead before Leonardo received an invitation from Francis I, "the king of the Renaissance," to take up his residence in France. Francis proved to be a generous patron. He had a sincere admiration for Leonardo, and treated him with consistent liberality and friendliness, granting him an annual pension and giving him the castle of Cloux, near Amboise, for a residence. More than that, the king himself paid frequent visits to Cloux. He also honoured Melzi, by conferring on him the honorary office of a Gentleman of the Bedchamber. At a later date, Francis expressed to Cellini his deep admiration for Leonardo, telling him that he did not believe that there had ever existed anyone who had so much knowledge as Leonardo possessed.

Amongst the visitors to Cloux, was the Cardinal of Aragon, whose secretary, Antonio de Beatis, in his *Itinerario*, gives an account of the visit. Leonardo "showed the Cardinal," he writes, "three pictures, one of a Florentine lady, done from life, on the instructions of the late Magnificent Giuliano de' Medici; another of St. John Baptist when young; and another of the Madonna and Child seated in the lap of St. Anne—all of them most perfect."[18]

Of the portrait here referred to nothing more is known. It is certainly not that of "Monna Lisa." For that picture was painted before the year 1506, at a time when Giuliano de' Medici was an exile and a wanderer, several years before he became Leonardo's patron. This "portrait of a Florentine lady" was probably begun by Leonardo during Giuliano's last period of residence in his native city in 1515 and 1516, and was not delivered by the artist, for the reason that his patron died

[18] L. Beltrami, *op. cit.*, p. 149.

before it was finished. It is not necessary to assume that the lady represented had been Giuliano's mistress.

Leonardo died at Cloux on May 2, 1519. Francis was then with the Court at St. Germain-en-Laye. Lomazzo tells us of his grief when he received, from the lips of Melzi, the news of his friend's death.

By his will, dated April 23, 1519, Leonardo left to his pupil, "Messer Francesco de' Melzi, gentleman of Milan," his books and manuscripts, as well as his drawings and other possessions. He made bequests to Salai and to his servant Battista de Villanis, to his brothers in Florence, to his serving-woman Matturina, to certain local charities, and to the poor of the locality. He directed that his body should be buried in the church of St. Florentin and that masses should be said for his soul in that church, as well as in the church of St. Dionysius at Amboise, and the church of the Friars Minor there.

In a letter that he wrote to Leonardo's brothers, Melzi tells them that "his master passed from this present life . . . . with all the rites of our Holy Mother Church, and well-prepared." He would never cease, he writes, as long as he lived, to mourn his "excellent father," who had daily shown him deep and ardent love.

Melzi proved himself to be a loyal friend of his dead master, whom he survived for fifty years. The villa at Vaprio became a shrine, and Melzi was its hierophant.

CHAPTER IV

MELZI'S HERITAGE

MELZI, we know, called Leonardo "father" and had more than a filial regard for his memory. The young artist had for his heritage all the collections that had belonged to his dead master—books of manuscripts and sketches, models and plaster figures, as well as some of his pictures, such as the "Virgin and Child and St. Anne," which Melzi brought back from Cloux to Vaprio.[1] In this bequest, too, was Leonardo's collection of his own cartoons, a collection that was made use of by Milanese followers of his, such as Marco d'Oggiono and Cesare da Sesto, Bernardino Luini and Salai, over a considerable period of time.

All that Melzi received from his dead master, by gift and by inheritance, he guarded carefully for half a century, until his death in 1570. At Vaprio, he was visited by Alberto Bendidio, the Duke of Ferrara's agent in Milan, by Lomazzo, himself a Milanese, and by Vasari, as well as by other writers, artists, and connoisseurs. To them he showed Leonardo's collections, and, from them, Vasari and Lomazzo obtained much valuable information about the master's life and works.

When Melzi died, all this was changed. His nephew, Orazio Melzi, did not prize or protect the treasures that he had inherited. He allowed them to lie neglected in the attics of the Melzi villa. As a consequence, some of the manuscripts were stolen by the family tutor, Lelio Gavardi. These were ultimately

---

[1] The best modern authorities for the history of the manuscripts are (1) J. P. Richter, *The Literary Works of Leonardo da Vinci* (2d ed. J. P. and Irma A. Richter; London and New York: Oxford University Press, 1939), II, 393–99; (2) G. Poggi, *Leonardo da Vinci, La Vita di Giorgio Vasari, Nuovamente Commentata e Illustrata*, etc. (Florence, 1919), pp. 47–63; and (3), for the history of the Windsor drawings, Kenneth Clark, *A Catalogue of the Drawings of Leonardo da Vinci, in the Collection of His Majesty the King, at Windsor Castle* (Cambridge University Press, 1936), pp. ix–xiv. For the chronology of the manuscripts, it is necessary to consult Girolamo Calvi, *I Manoscritti di Leonardo da Vinci dal punto di vista Cronologico, Storico e Biografico* (Bologna, 1925), and E. Solmi, "Le Fonti dei Manoscritti di Leonardo da Vinci" in *Giornale Storico della Letteratura Italiana* (Turin, 1908).

recovered, owing to the efforts of a Milanese lawyer, Giovanni Ambrogio Mazenta, who has left us an account of what happened to Francesco Melzi's heritage during the fifty years that followed his death.[2] When Mazenta returned the stolen manuscripts to Orazio Melzi,[3] the recipient expressed surprise that Mazenta had taken so much trouble about them and told him to keep them! After this circumstance became known to local collectors, many of them visited the Melzi villa, in the hopes of acquiring some of the Melzi treasures. The most persistent of these *pescatori* was Pompeo Leoni, the sculptor, who, after several years of effort, succeeded in getting into his possession, from different sources, by far the greater part of the original collection.[4] Rubens scarcely exaggerated when he testified that Pompeo Leoni had "all the studies and all the drawings that Leonardo had made."

Some of the volumes owned by Leoni, the sculptor cut into pieces, and made of them one large volume—a volume which came to be known as the *Codice Atlantico*. Finally, having been appointed official sculptor to the Court of Spain, he took with him to Madrid some small portion of his collection, with the intention of presenting it to his patron, Philip II. This plan, however, was not proceeded with. Leoni, there is reason to believe, retained practically the whole of his collection until his death at Madrid, when two of the volumes of Leonardo's manuscripts were included in the sale of his effects. It seems probable to me that he had left by far the greater part of his collection at his home in Milan.[5]

One of the volumes sold at Madrid—that which contained the priceless collection of drawings now at Windsor—was bought by Don Juan de Espinosa. Several years later, it was acquired by one of the world's great collectors, Thomas, Earl of Arundel, who, like Charles I, his royal master, was a passionate lover of the arts. Ultimately, this volume, after being lost for a long

---

[2] G. A. Mazenta, *Memorie dei fatti di Leonardo da Vinci e de' suoi Libri*, reprinted by G. Uzielli, in *Ricerche intorno a Leonardo da Vinci*, Ser. II (Rome, 1884), pp. 226–35. G. A. Mazenta died in 1635.

[3] J. P. and I. A. Richter, *op. cit.*, II, 394, 395.

[4] G. Poggi, *op. cit.*, p. 49; G. Paolo Lomazzo, *Idea del Tempio della Pittura* (1590), pp. 17, 18.

[5] Two volumes by Leonardo were once in the Royal Library at Madrid. See J. P. and I. A. Richter, *op. cit.*, II, 397, n.

period, was discovered by a Mr. Dalton, at the bottom of a chest in a royal palace in England, shortly after the accession of George III.[6]

It is certain that the great bulk of Pompeo Leoni's collection was inherited by his heir, Polidoro Calchi, and was sold by him, in 1625, to Count Galeazzo Arconati, the generous benefactor of the Ambrosian Library, who, eleven years later, presented to that institution twelve volumes of the manuscripts, amongst which was the *Codice Atlantico*. The collection in the Ambrosian Library was removed to Paris by Napoleon's order in 1796; and, of all the volumes then stolen, only the *Codice Atlantico* was ultimately returned to Milan.

Amongst the treasures that were bought by Arconati was Leonardo's collection of original cartoons. In all Melzi's heritage, there was no item of greater importance. In the second decade of the eighteenth century, the Arconati family decided to dispose of these cartoons; and they were sold to local collectors, the heads of Milanese noble families. The cartoons of Isabella d'Este and Monna Lisa were acquired, it seems, by the Marchese Calderara-Pino. Four other cartoons, we know, were purchased by the Marchese Casnedi. But little more than a century later, the cartoons of Monna Lisa and Isabella d'Este were bought by that remarkable connoisseur and collector of drawings, Giuseppe Vallardi of Milan, the head of a historic publishing house.

Vallardi regarded the portrait of Monna Lisa as the most important of all the drawings that he possessed. But when the cartoons were offered for sale, M. Reiset of the Louvre preferred the Isabella d'Este, because it was in a better state of preservation.

The importance of the Monna Lisa cartoon, however, continued to be recognized by art critics and art historians—by Ravaisson-Mollien and Salomon Reinach in a past generation, and by Suida and Bodmer in our own day.[7]

[6] Mary F. S. Hervey, *Thomas, Earl of Arundel* (Cambridge, 1921); Kenneth Clark, *Catalogue of the Drawings . . . . at Windsor Castle*, I, x–xiii.

[7] G. Vallardi, *Disegni di Leonardo da Vinci posseduti da G. Vallardi* (Milan: Tipografia di Pietro Agnelli, 1855); also the catalogue of the Vallardi Sale, Paris, December, 1860. S. Reinach, "La Tristesse de Mona Lisa," *Bulletin des Musées de France*, 1909, pp. 11–22; also S. Reinach, *Art*

The cartoons that the Marchese Casnedi acquired were of the highest importance. Fortunately, we possess a description of them by an English traveler, Edward Wright, tutor to Lord Parker, Viscount Ewelme, whom we have already quoted, who visited Milan in 1721, about a year after they had been added to the Casnedi collection.[8]

As this description of a part of Leonardo's collection of cartoons is of such great interest, we will reprint it here:

"The Marquis Casenedi, ... has a room entirely furnished with drawings, many very good. . . . . Those which are most admirable in the collection are cartones of Leonardo da Vinci, done in chalks, but raised a little higher with other crayons. . . . . Eleven of them are designs of all the heads and some of the hands of the *Last Supper* painted by him in fresco in the refectory of the Gratie, which is now in a manner spoiled. Two of these cartones contain two heads apiece; so that in the eleven cartones there are drawings of thirteen heads. The rest of his are as follows:—

A ritratt of the Duchess of Milan (Sforza).

Another ritratt, profile, without hands.

An old man resting his cheek on his left hand.

A Holy Family, the same which is painted in oil in the sacristy of S. Celsus.

A Leda standing,[9] naked, with cupids in one of the corners.

All these are by Leonardo da Vinci, and are as big as the life. . . . . These drawings of Leonardo da Vinci were purchased together by the Marquis for about three hundred pistoles, a year before we saw them, or thereabouts, of Count Alconati [*sic*] descendant of him who gave the volumes to the Ambrosian Library."

The first two drawings in this list were, it seems, cartoons for a portrait, or portraits, of Beatrice d'Este. The second of them

---

Journal, 1912, p. 6. G. Ravaisson-Mollien, "Le Carton de la Gioconde de la Collection Vallardi," *Bulletin de la Société Nationale des Antiquaires de France*, 1909, pp. 275, 276. Enrico Bodmer, *Disegni di Leonardo* (Florence: Sansoni, 1939), p. 17.

[8] Edward Wright, *Some Observations Made in Travelling through France and Italy . . . . in the Years 1720 and 1722* (London, 1730), pp. 470, 471.

[9] Note by E. Wright: "I think there is at Kensington, or in some of the King's Courts, one painted in much the same attitude."

may, in fact, have been a cartoon for the Castel-Pizzuto portrait. The third cartoon cannot be identified. The fourth is the cartoon of the "Virgin and Child and St. Anne" now at Burlington House. The last in the list is the cartoon for the "Leda," a picture which no longer exists, but of which, as we have already stated, there are copies by followers of Leonardo, at Wilton House and in the Borghese Gallery.

The Casnedi collection was sold in Venice some years later; and the cartoon of the "Virgin and Child and St. Anne" was bought, about 1760, by Robert Udny, the British consul in Venice. Ultimately, it came into the possession of the Royal Academy in London.

The *Trattato della Pittura* was not, of course, in the collection of original manuscripts of Leonardo, but was compiled out of some of them by Melzi or under his supervision. Many copies were made of it, for the most part very faulty and inaccurate; and several versions of it have been published since that of Raphael du Fresne in 1651. The best text of the *Trattato* is that which came to the Vatican Library from Urbino. This manuscript was published by Ludwig in 1882, and by Angelo Borzelli[10] in 1914. Professor Lionello Venturi is the author of a critical commentary on the *Trattato*.[11]

Melzi's heritage is now scattered about Europe; and portions of it are to be found in the libraries of Windsor and London, Paris, Milan, and Turin, as well as in such private libraries as those of Prince Trivulzio and the Earl of Leicester. Of Leonardo's large cartoons for painting, but three have survived. Such cartoons are perishable things, and, as a rule, they suffer much ill usage. The surviving cartoons are the "Isabella d'Este" of the Louvre, the "Monna Lisa," and the lovely drawing of the "Virgin and Child and St. Anne" at the Royal Academy.

It is in no small measure due to Giovanni Francesco Melzi that so many of Leonardo's manuscripts and drawings have come down to us. Italy has honored with memorials many men to whom it is far less indebted than it is to Leonardo's heir.

---

[10] H. Ludwig, *Lionardo da Vinci: Das Buch von der Malerei* ("Quellenschriften für Kunstgeschichte" [Vienna, 1882]); A. Borzelli, *Trattato della Pittura* (2 vols.; Lanciano, 1914).

[11] Lionello Venturi, *La Critica e l'Arte di Leonardo da Vinci* (Bologna, 1919).

CHAPTER V

LEONARDO AND THE CRITICS

ONE of the minor functions of the art critic is to endeavor to determine the authorship of those works of old masters whose origin is uncertain. Seventy years ago, that great critic Giovanni Morelli, introduced to the world a new method for arriving at correct attributions. That this method has proved of great value to connoisseurs cannot be denied. It soon became obvious, however, that it had its grave limitations, and that some of its early exponents were in danger of becoming heresiarchs. Possessing the virtues of the pioneer, they had also his accustomed failings. They were bigots, often lacking in a sense of proportion, who were prone to regard their guesses as established facts. Thus they came to believe, in true heretic fashion, that one method out of the whole corpus of appliances used by art critics was the only one that mattered very much. They attached too little importance to the evidence of contemporary documents, and to other sources of relevant information. They concentrated their attention on the often misleading and always incomplete evidence that a photograph could give them regarding a picture, neglecting the picture itself and giving too little attention to such important matters as color and artistic quality.[1] When I speak of quality, I include the more delicate shades of chiaroscuro, as well as those fine lines that do so much to make up what we call the *quality* of a picture, all of which are lost in the ordinary photograph of commerce.

This tendency to place too great reliance on the evidence of photographs has unfortunately increased in the present century, and more especially in the last decade. For, like all schismatics,

[1] L. Venturi, *Art Criticism Now* (Baltimore, 1941), p. 62:—"What is lacking in almost all the books and articles on art history today is the consciousness of the artistic result or quality of the work of art. . . . . The artistic quality of the work is generally overlooked by art historians."

the Morellians displayed a tendency to deteriorate. At one time, the leading exponents of Morellian doctrine refused to give an opinion on a picture that they had not seen. All this is changed now. In recent years, to my personal knowledge, some of these art critics have published opinions on pictures that they have never seen, and of which all the evidence that they possessed was derived from poor photographs taken many years before.

The reason for this declension is obvious, though unavowed. These students, if not rich themselves, had acquired the command of ample funds for their needs. It was no longer necessary, they argued, to acquire knowledge the hard way, as their elders had done, tramping long distances on dusty Italian roads, sleeping sometimes in a railway waiting-room in order to save the cost of a bed, lodging in primitive *locande* in small country towns, with the object of studying a few remote altarpieces in country churches, or to see a picture in a provincial gallery, when they could acquire the necessary knowledge from photographs, in their cosy studies, or in some art library. As for consulting documents in some distant archives—that was regarded as a sheer waste of time. Leave those dry bones to be mumbled by the doctors!

Nothing demonstrates more clearly the folly of undervaluing or neglecting documentary evidence than does the recent discovery of two documents that throw new light on Andrea del Castagno. It is not too much to say that these discoveries have revolutionized our ideas regarding his career as an artist, and his place in the history of Renaissance art. Earlier critics of Florentine painting, for example, believed that this so influential master was born in 1390, that he was a member, in fact, of that earlier generation of artists to which belonged Fra Angelico and Paolo Uccello, Masaccio and Masolino, Domenico Veneziano and Fra Filippo Lippi. We now know, from contemporary documents, that Castagno was not born until 1423, that he was, in fact, an artist of the second great period of transition, a contemporary of Alesso Baldovinetti and Antonio Pollajuolo.

We also know from documentary evidence published by Count Gamba that a picture of the "Assumption" in the Berlin

Gallery, a painting that had been given to minor artists of different schools by modern critics, is by Castagno. This is a most important discovery; as this dated work reveals relevant facts regarding the artist's development, and has already enabled students of his work to identify one other important picture from his hand, the Poggibonsi altarpiece—an altarpiece which because of its affinity in style to the "Assumption" from S. Miniato-fra-le-Torri, must have been painted between the years 1444 and 1450, and probably near 1450.

It is a significant fact that, in a country in which style-criticism had been more assiduously practiced than in any other, there had hung, for generations, in a great public gallery—a gallery frequented by leading art critics of Europe and America —a painting, the work of a great Italian master with a pronouncedly personal style, whose authorship these critics had altogether failed to determine, but which finally received its correct attribution from a student of "musty documents."

The fundamental weakness of the method of Morelli is, as has frequently been proved, that small morphological details can be reproduced with Chinese accuracy, both by a gifted, intelligent copyist and by a patient pupil. This fact can be demonstrated without going outside the critical writings published in the last seventy years regarding one artist—Leonardo da Vinci. Early in this period, a modern forgery, Donna Laura Minghetti's "Portrait of a Maiden," was pronounced by Morellians to be a work of this master, and "without an equal."[2] Today, the small "Annunciation" of the Louvre, a picture which, for nearly half a century, Morellian critics have described as the most perfect of the smaller paintings of the greatest of Italian masters, they now declare to be without doubt the work of that dull, third-rate artist, Lorenzo di Credi.

That the importance of the Morellian method, useful as it has proved to be, has been exaggerated by some critics of Italian painting is demonstrated by the fact that it is employed to so small an extent today—perhaps to too small an extent—by the

---

[2] B. Berenson, *The Drawings of the Florentine Painters of the Renaissance* (New York and London: G. P. Putnam & Sons, 1896), p. 66.

chief authorities on other schools of painting. It is easy, of course, for Morellians to retort by demonstrating the fallibility of all other methods than their own, and the inadequacy of other kinds of evidence than that which they regard as alone worthy of serious consideration. For the truth is that no method used by art critics is infallible, as connoisseurship is not, and cannot be, an exact science. For the art critic, as for the worker in so many other fields, "PROBABILITY IS THE GUIDE OF LIFE."

It may be contended that all these precepts of connoisseurship, that I have myself held and advocated for nearly fifty years, are now widely accepted; and that I am merely preaching to the converted. But there are still here and there, throughout Europe and in this country, small conventicles, in which foregather members of the strictest sect of Morellians, where hardshell elders impart to neophytes the narrow precepts of the orthodox Morellian creed.

In fact, the tendency of style-critics to study but one kind of evidence is still active, and has been the cause of unnecessary confusion and misunderstanding in the minds of students of the works of so great an artist as Leonardo. This is clear to those who read with attention recent writings on this master. The evidence that we possess in regard to Leonardo's activities is, for a great part of his career, by no means vague or scanty, if viewed in its entirety. For, in addition to the testimony that can be gleaned by the study of his drawings and pictures, as well as the statements in his own handwriting that are to be found on the leaves of Leonardo's sketchbooks, we have also the clear evidence of legal documents—sometimes, alas, garbled by partisan critics, and sometimes ignored—as well as the evidence of contemporary letter-writers and annalists, and the compilations of industrious chroniclers and biographers of the next generation, such as the Anonimo Gaddiano, Vasari, and Lomazzo, all of whom had the opportunity of consulting intimate friends of the artist, such as Francesco Melzi.

In weighing all the evidence, and more especially in estimating the importance of any piece of documentary evidence, we must, of course, first establish its authenticity, and then consider its relative value. And we must not exaggerate the importance of any part of it. But this unfortunately has not been done. Firsthand evidence of the highest authenticity has been passed over, whilst credence has been given to the testimony of some valueless document, when it seemed to lend weight to the conclusion of the writer. Critics who have not had a sound historical training often seem to be entirely incapable of assessing the value of documentary evidence. When they begin to realize that they have a poor case, they sometimes clutch at the testimony of some worthless piece of writing, just as a drowning man clutches at a floating sprit. I cannot help thinking that those neo-Morellians are wiser who make innumerable attributions, in weighty tomes, without giving their reasons! For their supposedly scientific conclusions are often purely subjective, the result of wishful thinking on the part of the critic.

Here I will only mention one instance of a conclusion based upon wholly inadequate documentary evidence—Berenson's statement in regard to the date of Lorenzo di Credi's birth. Credi, as we now know, was born in 1459 or 1460. This conclusion is based on unimpeachable testimony, the sworn deposition of his own mother.[3] In her Fiscal Declaration of 1480–81, which is in the Archivio di Stato at Florence, Credi's mother states that her son is twenty-one years of age. Had she, for some reason, wished to mislead the authorities, it would not have been possible for her to do so. For the Balducci family to which Credi belonged were no strangers to Florence. The artist's forebears had been known as goldsmiths in the city for some generations. Credi himself was a young apprentice in the most important studio there. It was easy, too, to check the accuracy of his mother's declaration by referring to the Register of Baptisms, or to Credi's articles of apprenticeship.

But those critics who put out the extraordinary theory that Credi was an infant prodigy feel now that it is necessary to make that theory a little more credible. They have sought, therefore, to show that Credi was in reality older than his own mother solemnly affirmed that he was. To do this they ignore alto-

---

[3] Archivio di Stato, Florence, *Portata al Catasto, 1480–1481*, Quart. di S. Spirito.

gether the Fiscal Declaration of Credi's parent, a document that is very damaging to their case. For not only does it state that Credi was then but twenty-one years old, it also shows that, in the year 1480, he occupied a very subordinate position in Verrocchio's studio. His mother testifies, in fact, that she and her son were living in poverty in two little rooms, and that Credi received from Verrocchio the miserable salary of twelve florins a year.[4] Disregarding, then, this declaration, they accepted, in complete good faith, as their chief authority for the date of Credi's birth an anonymous inscription on the back of a portrait in the Widener Collection, a portrait of disputed authorship. This inscription, which is admittedly not contemporary, and by an unknown hand, speaks of Credi as "un pittore eccelente," and states that, in 1488, he was thirty-two years of age. Surely it is a most unsatisfactory piece of documentary evidence! Yet it is this inscription that Berenson prefers to the sworn declaration of Credi's own mother. Writing on the subject of the Uffizi "Annunciation," he says: "Credi was born in 1456, and there is no reason for assuming that this picture was designed earlier than 1474, when he was eighteen, and quite old enough to act as Leonardo's assistant."[5]

Until eleven years ago, I believed that Morellian critics still held to the conviction that only one of Leonardo's early works had come down to us, the "Annunciation" of the Louvre. But, on seeing a copy of Berenson's *Italian Pictures of the Renaissance*, I realized that this distinguished critic had already made the journey to Canossa, and that he had at last admitted to the canon of Leonardo's works the three pictures which Morelli's chief opponent, Bode, long ago had attributed to Leonardo. These three paintings are the Uffizi "Annunciation," the Benois "Madonna," and the "Madonna and Child" at Munich. By attributing these works to Leonardo, Bode had earned the contempt of Morelli and his followers. Morelli, in fact, had declared that in giving the Munich "Madonna" to

[4] E. Müntz, *Chronique des Arts* (Paris, 1899), p. 312.

[5] B. Berenson, *The Drawings of the Florentine Painters of the Renaissance* (Chicago: 1938), I, 56; also *Italian Pictures of the Renaissance* (Oxford, 1932), p. 296.

Leonardo, Bode had "done an injury to the memory of the great Florentine."[6] Berenson, to his great credit, admitted freely and frankly his past errors in the last edition of his work on Florentine drawings.[7]

But the process of restoring to the list of Leonardo's works those pictures that are demonstrably by his hand has, in my opinion, not gone far enough. There is evidence to show that this great master was a far more prolific painter than the Morellians imagine him to have been. There is, in fact, abundant testimony to support this view in contemporary documents. But we will content ourselves with repeating here the evidence of one well-informed witness who knew the artist, Matteo Bandello, the *novelliere*, afterwards Bishop of Agen, who, in his youth, resided with his uncle, the Prior of the Convent of Santa Maria delle Grazie. In one of his *novelle*, Bandello tells a story about a friend of his. In doing so, he describes a certain apartment in his friend's palace, which was decorated with pictures by Leonardo. "Alcuni quadri," he writes, "di man di Mastro Lionardo da Vinci, il luogo mirabilmente adornavano."[8]

[6] G. Morelli, *Italian Painters* (London, 1900), II, 269.

[7] B. Berenson, *The Drawings of the Florentine Painters*, I, 56.

[8] M. Bandello, *Le Novelle* (Bari: G. Laterza, 1925), I, Novella III, p. 53. When Bandello tells us that "some pictures from the hand of Leonardo" adorned the walls of a palace in Milan, his evidence is of considerable importance. For his qualifications as a witness, see Appendix IV.

CHAPTER VI

LEONARDO'S PICTURES

THE FIRST FLORENTINE PERIOD. I

LEONARDO, as we have said, was primarily a painter. He regarded painting as the greatest of the arts, greater than sculpture, greater than poetry, greater even than music. It was in order that he might learn the art of painting that he entered Verrocchio's studio. It was as a painter that he worked with his master for ten years, helping him with such pictures as the "Baptism" of the Uffizi. At the early age of twenty-two he was enrolled in the Painters' Guild of Florence. Finally, as a painter of established reputation, he received an important commission from the State: he was intrusted with the task of painting an altarpiece for the Chapel of St. Bernard in the Palazzo della Signoria. It is unreasonable to suppose that an artist who was given so important a commission, and who, but three years later, created such a masterpiece as the Uffizi "Adoration" was not a painter with a large experience of his art. Nor was it only in Florence that Leonardo was regarded primarily as a painter. A patron of his later years, Charles d'Amboise, wrote of him that he was "famous in painting," and that he was "relatively little known in those other branches of knowledge in which he had reached so great a height."

Vasari's *Life* of Leonardo has always been regarded as one of the best of his biographies. A born story-teller, Vasari could not help interpolating two or three studio anecdotes; and, following the example of the hagiographers, he seeks to show that the subject of this *Life* began to display, at an early age, the singular gifts that God had given him. But, on the whole, he writes about the young Leonardo with considerable impartiality. He does not gloze over his chief failing—that innate instability of character that prevented the boy from profiting by the oppor-

49

tunities that he had for acquiring knowledge. Because of this failing Leonardo's progress in his chosen art was gradual. And undoubtedly the chief reason why his early works have not been generally recognized as his is that we find in them, here and there, certain imitative details, as well as many obvious imperfections.[1] Such was the reason, for example, why some critics excluded, for so long a time, the Uffizi ''Annunciation'' and the Benois ''Madonna'' from the Leonardo canon, paintings which, not without good reason, have been subjected to criticism.

It is, however, becoming more and more obvious that, although Leonardo was a genius, he did not suddenly spring upon the world fully equipped for his lifework. Like other great artists, he began by copying in many particulars the works of his master. In the landscape of the Dreyfus ''Madonna,'' for example, he was clearly influenced by such landscapes as those that we see in the background of the two pictures of the ''Madonna and Child'' by Verrocchio that are in Berlin, and the ''Madonna and Child'' by the same master that is in London. Verrocchio, as Sir Kenneth Clark has recently pointed out,[2] ''followed the current fashion, introduced through Flemish pictures and illuminated manuscripts, of round trees dotted about on a plain, with a horizon of rounded hills.'' In his landscapes ''everything is tidily arranged and sharply defined.'' Such a Verrocchiesque landscape we find in the Dreyfus ''Madonna,'' which is clearly Leonardo's earliest known work.

It is true, of course, that these landscapes of Verrocchio were also imitated by another pupil of his—Lorenzo di Credi—but with how great a difference! Credi soon standardized and vulgarized the kind of landscape that he had learned to paint in Verrocchio's studio until it became a tedious, lifeless convention. Leonardo, on the other hand, as his early drawings prove, looked upon the world with his own eyes. In or about

---

[1] B. Berenson, *The Drawings of the Florentine Painters* (Chicago, 1938), I, 56, 57; also E. McCurdy, *The Mind of Leonardo da Vinci* (London, 1928), p. 311. Frizzoni says of the Benois ''Madonna'' that it is ''not entirely successful if one admits certain obvious inequalities and imperfections.''

[2] *Leonardo da Vinci* (Cambridge, 1939), p. 13.

the year 1470 he began to evolve a new kind of landscape that was a presentation of his own vision of nature. We can detect, from that time onwards, the gradual emergence of a subtle and sensitive idiosyncrasy.

The subject that, more than any other, occupied Leonardo's mind in those early years was, as we have already stated, that of the Madonna and Child. In his sketchbooks were many drawings of this subject; and we soon begin to hear of several Madonnas that were painted by him. From an inscription written by the artist on a well-known drawing in the Uffizi,[3] we learn that, in the year 1478, he was engaged in painting two Madonnas. Some years later, in the list of his works in the *Codice Atlantico*, we read again of two pictures of the same subject, one of them "of Our Lady finished, another almost, in profile."[4] In time, Leonardo became widely known as a painter of small Madonnas. Isabella d'Este begs Fra Pietro da Novellara to persuade Leonardo to paint for her "a little picture of the Madonna, devout and sweet, as his wont."

Leonardo, we conclude, was a far more prolific painter than some critics have believed, and he must have painted several of these "little Madonnas." It is claimed that the Dreyfus "Madonna" is the earliest of these.[5] This picture is indeed a *little* Madonna; it is smaller than any other work of this kind that has been attributed to Leonardo, and it is also a painting of exquisite quality. We shall now proceed to show that it is by Leonardo da Vinci, and by no one else.

This panel has been attributed to Verrocchio; and certainly, since it is, as I believe, the earliest existing work of Leonardo, we must expect to find in it pronouncedly Verrocchiesque features, such as, for example, the landscape background to which we have already referred. In the painting of the Madonna

---

[3] H. Bodmer, *Leonardo, des Meisters Gemälde und Zeichnungen* ("Klassiker der Kunst" Series [Stuttgart, 1931]), p. 115.

[4] Kenneth Clark, *op. cit.*, pp. 40–44.

[5] The Dreyfus "Madonna" was first published by J. Guiffrey in *Les Arts*, 1908, No. 71. It was attributed to Leonardo by Suida in his book, *Leonardo und sein Kreis* (Munich, 1929); by Degenhart in the *Rivista d'Arte*, October and December, 1932; and by myself in my book *Leonardo da Vinci: His San Donato and the Tax Collector* (London, 1932), p. 8.

herself Leonardo seems to have been influenced to some extent by a lost drawing[6] by Verrocchio, of which there is a fine early copy in the Dresden Gallery. It seems that considerable use was made of the original drawing in the master's studio.[7]

But, viewed as a whole, the Dreyfus "Madonna" differs *au fond* from any representation of the Madonna by Verrocchio. In that master's painting of this subject, the relation between the Mother and the Child is still expressed in the same way as it is in the works of such naturalist painters of the middle of the century as Fra Filippo Lippi and Alesso Baldovinetti— painters who had been influenced by such contemporary sculptors as Desiderio da Settignano. In their pictures of the Madonna, the Blessed Virgin is detached, remote; she displays but little maternal feeling. Leonardo, on the other hand, in this picture, as in his early drawings, emphasizes—as Donatello had done—the human relationship between the Mother and the Infant. The Blessed Virgin, as Suida points out,[8] draws the Child to her side and spreads her own cloak on the parapet on which the Child stands, to protect his feet from the cold stone.

This picture has also been attributed to Lorenzo di Credi, an attribution far less excusable than that which gave it to Verrocchio. For there is nothing so difficult to understand, in the whole history of modern art criticism, as the attempt to prove that "this mediocre painter, in whose work we can trace no development from his twenty-fifth year," was indeed a youthful portent.

In a series of articles, published in the *Rivista d'Arte* in 1932, Degenhart set out to prove that Credi was a prodigy, who produced more works of some importance before attaining the age of twenty-one than any other Italian master succeeded in doing. He claims that, before the year 1481, Credi had painted the following ten pictures: The Dresden "Madonna" (No. 13), the "Virgin Adoring the Child" at Dresden (No. 14), the Berlin

[6] W. von Bode, *Studien über Leonardo da Vinci* (Berlin, 1921), Fig. 10; W. Suida, *op. cit.*, p. 17; B. Berenson, *op. cit.*, Vol. III, Fig. 139.

[7] It is uncertain who made this sensitive, subtle copy of the lost drawing, but most assuredly it is not by such a heavy-handed mediocrity as Credi.

[8] *Op. cit.*, p. 17.

"Madonna" (in part), the Strasbourg "Madonna," the "Madonna" of the London National Gallery (No. 648), a "Madonna" at Mainz, a "Madonna" at Karlsruhe, a lost "Madonna" painted from a design in the Albertina Collection, "The Assumption of St. Louis" in the Huntington Collection, at San Marino, California, a portrait now at Forlì.

Berenson went even further than Degenhart in the effort to prove that Credi was a youthful marvel. In the same year in which Degenhart's articles appeared, he claimed that Credi, who, as we know, was born in 1459 or 1460, had painted a part of the Uffizi "Annunciation"—a picture which he now attributes to Leonardo—in the years 1474 and 1475, that is to say when he was fourteen or fifteen years of age. More than this, he attributed that small masterpiece, the Louvre "Annunciation," to the young Credi, and asserted that it was painted by him in or about the very year in which Credi's mother had declared that her son was a poor apprentice in Verrocchio's studio, in receipt of a miserable wage of twelve florins a year.

Until Degenhart's articles were published, expert opinion was almost unanimous in its judgment of Lorenzo di Credi. As an average sample of the opinions expressed of him and his work by critics of the last generation, we quote the following, by the author of an admirable monograph on Verrocchio: "No imitator has done more to injure his master's reputation than Credi; for while copying certain of Verrocchio's outward forms, he has entirely effaced in those forms any trace of his energy and distinction. Certain realisms of structure he has exaggerated into unpleasant mannerisms, vulgarizing everything he touches with his temperamental feebleness. Feebleness and vulgarity must have been ineradicable in his nature, since a lifetime spent in the society of such men as Leonardo and Verrocchio was not sufficient to eliminate these defects. . . . . He . . . . remained to the last, too, ... the same crude and commonplace colourist. No spark of genius was ever struck from him."[9]

This paragraph records the orthodox doctrine regarding Lorenzo di Credi, as it was taught in the Morellian academies in the

[9] M. Cruttwell, *Verrocchio* (London, 1904), p. 208.

closing years of the last century. And nothing that has come to light since then has modified our opinion of this artist.

It may be urged that Credi, like some other pupils of great artists—such as, for example, Rembrandt's pupil, Nicholas Maes—excelled himself in his early years when he worked with that master. But this theory cannot hold water when we take into account all that we know of Credi's personality. Maes was always developing, always in movement. In his later period, it is true, he worshiped false gods, being too much under the influence of current French fashions; but, though he sometimes advanced in the wrong direction, he did not show himself incapable of learning. Credi, on the other hand, had a static temperament. Having acquired, after a long and slow development, some control of the means of expression, he could not do anything but make manifest his own commonplace personality. Looking at the earliest of his works, we can easily comprehend why it was that he occupied so mean a position in Verrocchio's studio when he was already twenty-one years of age. With these pictures before us, it is impossible to believe that he was capable at any time of executing a work of such distinction, of such rare and subtle quality, as the Dreyfus "Madonna."

Berenson evidently realizes, in some measure, the objections that will naturally be raised against the attribution that he has made. For, in his article in the *Bollettino d'Arte*, which he reprints in his *The Drawings of the Florentine Painters of the Renaissance*,[10] he reiterates, in different words, the statement that the Dreyfus "Madonna" is a faithful copy of a lost work by Leonardo. "This Madonna," he says, is "a schematic version of a Leonardo, lost, and antecedent to any known painting." It is, he says, "the closest imitation of a vanished Leonardo." It is "a simplified copy of a Madonna and Child" of the great master, "by the adolescent Lorenzo di Credi." It seems, too, that he can name certain morphological details in which, as he believes, the hand of Credi is revealed. In doing this, he exposes still further the weakness of his case. For the chief details that he selects are the hair and the eyes of the Madonna, thus

[10] I, 66, 67.

choosing, as we shall presently show, some of the elements of
the picture that are peculiarly characteristic of Leonardo himself.

Leonardo, as we can see from his generally accepted works,
painted different kinds of hair. Sometimes he gives us a heavy
tangled mass of hair: at other times, as in the portrait at Cracow
and the portrait of Ginevra dei Benci, it has a more or less trim
simplicity. Not always did he paint such hair as Berenson so
eloquently describes. Not always does he represent "a fascinat-
ingly labyrinthine arrangement with the strands twisted and
tangled and knotted, yet each hair keeping as it were, on its
own lyrical course, drawn out, to the highest note."[11]

Now in the Dreyfus picture the hair is treated with considerably less simplicity than it is in some of the generally accepted works of Leonardo's first period; it is certainly as
vital as it is in any of them. Each single hair, in fact, has a
certain animate quality. No photograph does justice to this
very characteristic hair of Leonardo. For, in every photograph,
some of these subtle filaments are altogether lost. I will, therefore, support my personal testimony as to the quality of the
hair in the Dreyfus "Madonna" by the evidence of Degenhart,
who, Crediphile though he be, confesses that this little picture
is too fine in quality for the subject of his untiring researches.
"The very fact," he writes, "that in the Dreyfus *Madonna* you
may discern these delicate liberties in the construction of the
hair—*of which a reproduction cannot give an idea* owing to its
minuteness—makes it possible with certainty to give the picture to Leonardo and not to Lorenzo di Credi."[12]

Berenson also regards the eyes of the Madonna in the Dreyfus
picture as peculiarly characteristic of Lorenzo di Credi. He
claims that he recognizes "in the pupil of the eye, visible between half-closed eyelids, a mannerism which is without doubt
characteristic of Credi and his imitators." But an eye drawn in
this way is also to be found in the undisputed works of Leonardo, as well as in the pictures of several of his Milanese followers.

[11] *Ibid.*, I, 66.
[12] B. Degenhart, *op. cit.*, p. 405. The italics are mine.

We find it, for example, in the "St. Anne" in Leonardo's altar-piece in the Louvre; in the Munich "Madonna"; in the Child of the Benois "Madonna"; in the school version of "The Madonna with the Yarn-Winder," which is in the Duke of Buccleuch's collection; in Melzi's "Columbine," now in Leningrad; as well as in certain "Madonnas" by Bernardino de' Conti, Marco d'Oggiono, Sodoma, and Luini. The truth is that it is not possible to find in the Dreyfus "Madonna" a single detail which is not characteristic of the young Leonardo.

It is interesting to note that the Virgin's cloak is fastened with a morse—a large cornelian surrounded by a border of pearls—a jewel similar to that which we find in several other works of the master, such as the Munich "Madonna"; the drawing for the head of this Madonna, which is in the Louvre; the Benois "Madonna"; the "Virgin of the Rocks"; and the "San Donato of Arezzo and the Tax Collector," as well as in a terra-cotta relief of the Madonna by Leonardo's master, which is now in the Bargello.[13]

Leonardo in this picture, the earliest of all his known paintings, emphasizes, for the first time in this medium, the intimate human relationship of the Mother and the Child—a relationship which this great humanist artist returns to again and again, in his early drawings. For the first time, too, he paints the strangely vital hair that we find in his greatest works. This, in fact, is the earliest existing product of that amazing constructive imagination, so restless, so prolific, whose possessor was a pioneer, far in advance of his own generation and of several succeeding generations in many fields of human activity, but who most completely expressed himself in the art of painting.[14]

Vasari's statement that Verrocchio never touched a brush, after he had seen the Angel that his young pupil painted in the "Baptism of Christ," is just the kind of exaggeration that a born

---

[13] This ornament is also to be found in the deplorable version of the Pistoia altarpiece, a work, in part, of Credi's school, which is at Naples.

[14] The attribution of this picture to Leonardo is singularly confirmed by a study of the ultra-violet-ray photograph of the picture. The drawing that was the basis of this little picture has a force, as well as a subtle, sensitive fineness, that is beyond anything that Credi was capable of.

raconteur—always on the look-out for a story—habitually
makes. Like certain journalists of our popular press, he could
not help embellishing his picture, by accentuating a line or two
here and there, and by painting into it a few flowers of sentiment
to give it color. And yet, beneath Vasari's tallest stories, there
usually is—as is the case in the productions of our more scrupu-
lous contemporary annalists—a sound substratum of truth. The
"Baptism" is not a great picture; but by far the best part of it
is by Leonardo.

That this painting is later in date than the Dreyfus picture is clear. For, in that part of it which Leonardo painted,
the pupil is less under the dominating influence of his master
than he was when he created the tiny "Madonna" of his youth.
In the "Baptism," Leonardo reveals more of his own personal
style—in the hair of the Angel on the left of the picture, in the
drapery of that figure, and in the landscape, which, we believe,
was finished by the younger artist. The loose, tumbling hair of
this Angel, full of vitality, and light and shade, reminds us, as we
look at it, of somewhat similar hair that the master painted in a
later time—in the "Virgin of the Rocks," and in the portrait of
Beatrice d'Este.

The sharp folds of the drapery recall to us Vasari's account of
the methods of the youthful artist. "Because he wished to be a
painter," Vasari writes, "he studied much in drawing from
nature. Making models, too, of figures in clay, he covered them
with soft old linen which had been dipped in water mixed with
clay. He then set himself to draw, with great patience, on a
kind of fine Rheims cloth, or prepared linen. And these drawings
which he executed in black and white, with the point of a
brush, are indeed marvellous; as some of them which are in
my book of drawings can still testify."

In the third place, in the landscape of the "Baptism" we find
evidence of the growth of a personal style. It differs from the
neat landscape of the Dreyfus "Madonna," in which Leonardo
imitated—and surpassed—his master. His individual treatment
of landscape began early; and, but two or three years after he
had painted his share of the "Baptism," it reached a remarkable

stage of development, as can be seen by looking at the well-known drawing of the Arno Valley.

The "Annunciation" of the Uffizi, is, as we have stated elsewhere, a composite work. For this reason, it has been attributed to several different artists—to Verrocchio, to Domenico Ghirlandajo, to Ridolfo Ghirlandajo, and even to Credi. This last humiliation it really does not deserve. For, notwithstanding its glaring faults, it is a work of great charm—as full, in fact, of magic and freshness as any other picture of Leonardo, except the Louvre "Annunciation" and the cartoon of the "Virgin and Child and St. Anne" at Burlington House.

The attribution to Verrocchio, like the attribution to Ghirlandajo, has some justification. The general design of the whole work was probably made by Verrocchio, the head of the studio. But Leonardo certainly painted the figure of the Angel Gabriel, and by far the greater part of the rest of the picture. Then, as he did in so many cases, he left the job unfinished. The Virgin Annunciate was brushed in, I believe, by his fellow-pupil, Domenico Ghirlandajo, painting under Leonardo's direct influence. And the same artist painted the incongruous reading-desk, at a time when he had but little knowledge of the laws of perspective.

Ghirlandajo was an artist who excelled in painting portraits of the wives of successful men. His Virgin Annunciate is no virgin and no saint. She reminds me of nothing more than a pleasant, worldly hostess of the plutocracy, who, on a Sunday, receives her husband's friends in a country home on Long Island or in a modernized manor-house in Surrey. "So pleased to see you," I can hear her say. As for the design of the drapery that covers her legs, which I once took exception to in a Court of Justice, I still think that my description of it did not err on the side of severity. I have discovered since then, on reading Thiis' book on Leonardo, that this excellent critic has much the same opinion of this drapery as I then expressed.[15]

[15] J. Thiis, *Leonardo da Vinci: The Florentine Years of Leonardo and Verrocchio* (London, n.d. [?1914]), p. 101.

A picture belonging to the same period as the Uffizi "Annunciation," but later in date, is the portrait of Ginevra dei Benci in the Liechtenstein Gallery at Vienna. It is not necessary to repeat here the obvious reasons for believing that this is the portrait of Ginevra dei Benci mentioned by Vasari. Reasons of style, however, point to the conclusion that, contrary to Vasari's statement, it is an early work, probably painted soon after Ginevra's marriage in 1474. We must be on our guard against speaking in terms of exaggerated praise of any of these early pictures because they happen to be by Leonardo. This picture, however, has one great merit: It is clean. And because it is clean, we can observe all those faint, subtle gradations of light and shade in the painting of the flesh which count for so much and of which a photograph tells us too little. It is interesting to note how the over-full lower lip of the young woman contradicts her demure expression, her cold observant eyes, and her primly ordered locks. The beautiful landscape, too, with its deep shade, and its mysterious pool of water, is an advance on the landscapes of his earlier paintings. But, having conceded all this, and having taken into account the fact that it has been mutilated, it cannot be admitted that this is one of the world's masterpieces: It is a promising work, by a young artist of genius. There are several such portraits in the world. And this is the reason why it has been given to Verrocchio, and to other masters, by discerning critics. I must confess that even today—and I saw the picture quite recently—it leaves me quite cold. I do not believe, as some hold, that the hands were originally shown in this somewhat mutilated portrait; and I cannot agree that the "Study of Hands" at Windsor (No. 12.558) is of nearly so early a date as the "Ginevra dei Benci."[16]

Another picture of Leonardo's early period, the period when he was a follower of Verrocchio, but was gradually evolving a personal style, is the Munich "Madonna and Child." Owing to the fact that it is obviously a product of Verrocchio's workshop,

[16] P. Müller-Walde, *Leonardo da Vinci: Lebenskizze und Forschungen* (Munich, 1889–90), p. 52; W. von Bode, "Leonardos Bildnis der jungen Dame mit dem Hermelin aus dem Czartoryski Museum in Krakau und die Jugenbilder des Kunstlers," *Jahrbuch*, XXXVI (1915), 204.

it has been given by some critics to Lorenzo di Credi. Because the most important parts of the picture have been overpainted in an oil medium and consequently have a suspicious *craquelure*, it has been pronounced by other critics to be an old copy. But it is very clearly a work of Leonardo; and it is full of details that recall to us other works of the master.[17] Certainly, the design of the figure of the Madonna is based on the school copy of a drawing by Verrocchio which is at Dresden, to which we have already referred. The original drawing was used by Verrocchio himself, when he painted, a little later, the "Madonna di Piazza." It seems to have been a popular drawing in the studio; as it was also used, and probably copied, by more than one of Verrocchio's pupils.[18]

In three details in the Munich "Madonna," we can see unmistakably the hand of Leonardo. In the first place, in the gestures of the Child, as well as in the left hand of the Virgin, this picture reminds us of an earlier work of Leonardo—the Dreyfus "Madonna." Secondly, the sharp, clear-cut folds of the Virgin's cloak, a part of which lies on her lap, are very characteristic of Leonardo. Thirdly, the extraordinary landscape, revealing the artist's love of high mountain peaks, is a feature that does not reappear in his paintings until nearly thirty years later, when, inspired by his memories of the High Alps as seen from the Valtellina and the Upper Engadine, he painted the background of the portrait of "Monna Lisa." Finally, the whole picture, as it now is, with all its humiliating weaknesses and disguises, tells me in unmistakable tones that it is the work of a master and that it is not the offspring of one of the common herd of artists.

[17] The Munich "Madonna," attributed to Leonardo by Bayersdorfer, Bode, Suida, and other critics of Italian painting, has now been admitted to the list of Leonardo's authentic works by Berenson.

[18] There is, too, in the Louvre, a drawing for the head of the Madonna by Leonardo himself. It is reproduced in W. Suida, *op. cit.*, Pl. 4.

CHAPTER VII

LEONARDO'S PICTURES

THE FIRST FLORENTINE PERIOD. II

THAT great altarpiece, the "Madonna di Piazza," hangs in the Cathedral of Pistoia. It is complete except for its predella. The three scenes that composed the predella are now separated. One of them is in the Louvre, another in the Museum at Worcester, Massachusetts, whilst a third, which is by Perugino,[1] is in the Liverpool Gallery.[2] This altarpiece is the only really documented picture by Verrocchio; and it was painted, as we shall see, when Leonardo was head of the department of painting in Verrocchio's studio, and when Perugino, who owed so much to Verrocchio, was also at work there.[3] It therefore merits much more consideration than it has hitherto received.

In the center of the picture the Madonna is represented seated, on a throne of classical design. On the Virgin's right stands St. John the Baptist, on her left an episcopal saint, whom I identified in the year 1932 as S. Donato of Arezzo,[4] this figure having been regarded, up to that date, as a representation of S. Zeno or S. Zenobio. The subjects of the three predella panels, as is natural, are taken from the lives of the Blessed Virgin, S. Donato of Arezzo, and St. John the Baptist.

Morelli, with his remarkable flair and his keen eye for morphological details, gave us adequate reasons for his conclusion that the "Madonna di Piazza" was by Verrocchio, and that the Louvre "Annunciation" (which we now know to be

[1] B. Berenson, *Pitture Italiane del Rinascimento* (Milan, 1936), p. 376.

[2] This picture was identified by Valentiner, in 1942, as the third panel of the predella of the Pistoia altarpiece. He has generously permitted me to be the first to publish this interesting discovery.

[3] G. Vasari, *Le Vite*, ed. G. Milanesi (Florence, 1878–85), III, 371 and 568.

[4] R. Langton Douglas, *Leonardo da Vinci: His San Donato and the Tax Collector* (London, 1933), pp. 9 and 10.

a part of the predella of that altarpiece) was by Verrocchio's chief assistant, Leonardo da Vinci. Subsequently, these attributions of the great critic have been confirmed by the discovery of important documents in the Pistoia Archivio, and by other documentary evidence. We now know, from the testimony of these contemporary documents, the early history of the *ancona*.

We know, for instance, from a letter written at the bidding of the Operai of the Duomo of Pistoia in 1485, that Verrocchio had been commissioned to paint an altarpiece for the Chapel of the Sacrament in the cathedral, by the executors of Bishop Donato de' Medici, after that prelate's death in 1474.[5] We know, too, that the artist supplied the Bishop's executors with a description of the proposed altarpiece and a complete design for it. The whole work, in fact, and not a mere part of it had been "almost finished" at some date in 1478, or early in 1479; indeed there are now some definite grounds for the conclusion that the predella was painted in 1477.

The panel of the predella, which is in the Worcester Museum, represents, as we have said, a scene from the legend of S. Donato of Arezzo.[6] The incident is thus described by the saint's biographers. A tax collector, a certain Eustatius, had been falsely suspected of stealing sums of money paid to him in taxes. The supposed thief appealed to S. Donato, Bishop of Arezzo, explaining to him that, whilst he was away from home, his wife, Euphrosyne, had concealed the money, and had died before his return, leaving no record as to where it was hidden. S. Donato went at once to the woman's tomb with the widower. Kneeling down, he prayed for help from God, and then called out: "Euphrosyne! by Christ crucified, I conjure you to tell us what you have done with the money." Whereupon, a voice replied, telling the saint where the money was hidden. In this predella panel, we see the

[5] Archivio Comm. di Pistoia, Cod. 68, N. 684. Transcribed and published by A. Chiti in the *Bollettino Storico Pistoiese*, Vol. I, Fasc. 2 (1899); see also M. Cruttwell, *Verrocchio* (London, 1904), pp. 254, 255. A. Chiappelli contributed an important article to the *Bollettino d'Arte* (XII [1925], 54–65), in which he related the history of the "Madonna di Piazza." See Appendix I.

[6] S. Donato of Arezzo is not to be confounded with another Tuscan saint, S. Donato of Fiesole. For particulars of S. Donato of Arezzo's life see R. P. Fr. Laurentius Surius, *De Probatis Sanctorum Vitis* (Cologne, 1618), III, 90; also A. Albergotti, *De Vita et Cultu S. Donati Arretinae Ecclesiae Episcopi et Martiris* . . . . (8vo; Arezzo, 1782), of which an Italian translation was published at Lucca in 1785; also P. Buonamico, *Discorso sopra la vita di S. Donato Vesc. d'Arezzo* . . . . (Firenze, 1607).

Bishop kneeling in prayer, whilst Eustatius points to the open grave.

The representation of the saint in the rediscovered panel is similar to that of him in the upper portion of the altarpiece which is still at Pistoia, in form, garb, and features. Moreover, in both representations of the saint, we find a close resemblance to the portrait bust of the Bishop Donato de' Medici, which is in the same chapel.

In the predella panel, the saint and the widower are presented kneeling, facing each other, in the portico of a church or Campo Santo. The open tomb is between them. From the small figure of the angel-messenger, a ray of light strikes down to the heart of the kneeling Bishop. Through the portico are seen the trees of a garden, with distant hills beyond. The predominant colors are a warm brown and an olive-green. The cope of the kneeling Bishop is of a dull plum color, and has a dark golden lining. It is fastened with a morse consisting of a large red cornelian with a few pearls round it.—A similar jewel, as we have already seen, is to be found in several other early works of Leonardo.—The widower's cloak is an orange-yellow. The trees in the background are dark, as in the "Annunciation," silhouetted against a pale blue sky. But, here and there, in their foliage are tiny specks of gold, where the gold ground shines through. In the foreground and in the middle distance, the prevailing color, as in the "Virgin of the Rocks," is of a golden brown.

Valentiner's identification of the third panel of the predella, the "Birth of St. John the Baptist," is important for two reasons. It throws some light on Perugino's early career as an artist, and it helps us to fix the date of the predella of the "Madonna di Piazza."

Perugino's latest biographer, Fiorenzo Canuti, is of the opinion that Perugino was at work in Verrocchio's studio from 1472 to 1478,[7] except during a brief period of absence in 1475, when, we know, he paid a visit to Perugia. In any case it is certain that Verrocchio's pupil and assistant was absent from the summer

---

[7] Fiorenzo Canuti, *Il Perugino* (Siena, 1931), I, 34. Canuti's book is indispensable to all students of Perugino's works.

of 1475 to 1478, and that he left Florence early in the latter year because of disturbances in that city, and because of strained relations between the governments of Florence and Perugia. The works that we know Perugino executed in the years following 1477 were the fresco of St. Sebastian at Cerqueto, painted in 1478, and the "Delivery of the Keys" in the Sistine Chapel, which was painted in 1482. These frescoes clearly reveal the influence of Verrocchio, to whom, according to Vasari, Perugino owed his education as an artist.

With this statement of the Aretine biographer, modern critics, relying on the evidence afforded by the master's early works, are in entire agreement.[8] "Of Verrocchio's influence on Perugino," writes Miss Cruttwell, "there are unmistakable signs in the earlier works of the Umbrian painter, particularly in the *Delivery of the Keys* in the Cappella Sistina, which was painted in 1482. . . . . Here we find not only the features of the Christ," as we see them in Verrocchio's masterpiece, the bronze group of "Christ and St. Thomas" at Or San Michele, but also "the entire figure of St. Thomas, which is reproduced with little variation" in the representation of St. John the Evangelist.[9] Thus it is clear that Perugino had seen the clay model of the "Christ and St. Thomas," which was in his master's *bottega* at the time that he was working there.

The altarpiece, the "Madonna di Piazza," occupied Verrocchio and his chief assistants, at intervals, from 1474 or 1475 to 1478. Verrocchio, it seems, had arranged that Leonardo, the head of his *bottega*, should paint the predella of this important picture, a work that had been commissioned by the executors of a member of the ruling family in Florence. But, with his usual variability, Leonardo left the task unfinished after painting two of the panels. He then intrusted the completion of the predella to his commercially-minded colleague, who, more than once in his career, was summoned to finish a work that his friend had begun.[10] It seems clear, then, that the predella

---

[8] B. Berenson, *op. cit.*, p. 374.   [9] M. Cruttwell, *op. cit.*, p. 206.

[10] The companion panel at Worcester is of almost the same height as the "St. John the Baptist," but not of the same width. This is due to the fact that the broad border which was painted on each of the three panels of the predella has been cut away from each side of the Worcester picture.

of the "Madonna di Piazza" was finished in 1477 or very early in 1478.

Verrocchio, indeed, had been, for him, unusually speedy in carrying out this commission; and his clients were more than satisfied with what he had done. The document states that the altarpiece is "a very beautiful thing, that it had been brought to its present point with great art, ... and that it would undoubtedly prove to be an honour and ornament to the city, and an aid to devotion." Its actual completion, however, had been delayed for more than six years, owing to the fact that the Bishop's executors had not paid Verrocchio certain instalments of the total cost that were due to him.

The Operai called upon Verrocchio, in 1485, to complete the work that he had undertaken, in accordance with his original description and design; and they agreed that they would then pay the artist the sums that were due to him. On receipt of this letter, Verrocchio, who had left for Venice to create the most important work of his life, the Colleoni statue, arranged that his assistant, Lorenzo di Credi, who had recently been put in charge of his studio, should complete the almost finished altarpiece.

We also know certain other relevant facts that throw some light on the earlier history of the "Madonna di Piazza." We learn, for example, from an inscription in Leonardo's handwriting on a drawing of his that was made in 1478—the "Study of Two Heads" in the Uffizi[11]—that the artist was in Pistoia in that year, that is to say about the time that the altarpiece was "almost finished."

Thus Morelli's critical acumen was justified by unimpeachable documentary evidence. In view of all the facts, I had arrived long ago at the inevitable conclusion that the "Madonna di Piazza," like the Uffizi "Annunciation," was a composite work; that it was in part painted by Verrocchio, who was aided by his chief assistant, Leonardo, and also by Perugino; and that, after an interval of more than six years, the altarpiece received some finishing touches from Credi, the industrious but backward

[11] See A. Venturi, *I Manoscritti e Disegni di Leonardo....* (Rome: R. Comm. Vinc., 1930), Fasc. II, Pl. XXXIII; also G. Calvi, *I Manoscritti di Leonardo da Vinci* (Bologna, 1925).

apprentice, who had at last been rewarded for his personal devotion to his master by being placed at the head of the studio, when Verrocchio had finally taken a house in Venice.

I claim no originality for these conclusions of mine in regard to the Pistoia altarpiece. Nearly thirty years ago, Jens Thiis, in his important work on the early period of Leonardo, arrived at the same conclusions. "Undoubtedly," he writes, "Verrocchio commenced it, and even carried it on to the 'almost finished' condition in which it stood in 1478. And we may assume that he intended to complete it himself, otherwise there is no good reason why the picture should have been set aside for more than six years. If Verrocchio had intrusted his apprentice Credi with the completion of the altarpiece, he would not have allowed the pupil to idle over it for six whole years, particularly as the payment of the sum still due for the picture depended only on its completion. If Credi became responsible for the picture, why did not the Pistoians remind him of it? They must have known him. He had lived in their midst. If any reliance can be placed on contemporary documents, the Chiti document settles the question, and the Pistoian altarpiece is a work by Verrocchio, to which Credi gave the final touches when the cathedral authorities became insistent in 1485 and demanded the picture. It is possible that he did not deliver it until after Verrocchio's death in 1488. In this way, Credi's name has become associated with the altarpiece, an example of the manner in which incorrect but quite plausible traditions may be formed."[12]

Having accepted these conclusions, some of us fondly imagined that all the controversies that had raged in regard to the authorship of the "Madonna di Piazza" were now settled. The picture, we thought, could be justifiably attributed to Verrocchio. For it was as much his work as most of the larger paintings of Rubens—pictures that are to be seen in such galleries as the Louvre and the Antwerp Museum—are the work of Rubens, and as many famous pictures that bear the name of Van Dyck are the work of that artist. It is, certainly, as much the work of Verrocchio as many works of the British School, from the days

---

[12] J. Thiis, *Leonardo da Vinci: The Florentine Years of Leonardo and Verrocchio* (London, n.d. [1913]), p. 120.

of Sir Joshua Reynolds to our own age, are the actual handiwork
of the artists in whose studios they were painted. Those of us
who have frequented artists' studios in the last fifty or sixty
years could give some pertinent evidence on this point!

In support of our contention that Morelli was right in
attributing this picture to Verrocchio, we can quote the considered testimony of Berenson himself. He has told us that when
a critic is "fortified with the experience of the artist at his
highest . . . . he may well afford to relax, and include," in the
list of that artist's pictures, "every work that shows distinct
traces of his creative purpose, whether largely, or only in small
part by his own hand, ... or whether done in his studio on
his indications. . . . . An artistic personality includes not only
all that the artist did in his best moments, but all that his mind
conceived in the terms of his art, in whatever shape it has been
recorded, no matter how inadequate, nor how unsatisfactory."[13]

Surely, if this rule be followed in giving attributions—as I
believe that it ought to be—the main part of the altarpiece must
be given, as Morelli maintained, to Verrocchio. In designing the
predella, on the other hand, Verrocchio clearly allowed his
brilliant colleague, Leonardo da Vinci, more freedom than he
would have given some junior apprentice.

Our conclusion that the controversies about the "Madonna
di Piazza" were at an end was soon to be shattered. In the year
1938, after the discovery of a second panel of the predella of the
"Madonna di Piazza"—a picture which unfortunately Berenson
had never seen at the time that he wrote about it—that distinguished critic changed his opinion regarding the altarpiece
at Pistoia. He maintains now that it is not a composite picture,
as he had once held,[14] but that it is entirely the work of Credi.
Nay more, he now says that the Louvre "Annunciation"—the
very picture which for more than sixty years not only Morel-

[13] B. Berenson, *Italian Pictures of the Renaissance* (Oxford: Clarendon Press, 1932), pp. iii and iv.

[14] B. Berenson, *The Drawings of the Florentine Painters of the Renaissance* (London: John Murray,
1903), I, 45: "I find the Baptist in the painting greatly superior, not only to the drawing, but to the
rest of the painting, and to any other picture that can be ascribed to Credi. I seem to observe in
that one figure of the Baptist, a largeness and puissance of modelling, and in the head a character
that I can only account for on the supposition that Verrocchio himself had greatly cooperated on
this figure."

lians but all the leading critics of Italian painting had recognized to be a little masterpiece of Leonardo's early time—is the work of that same mediocre artist, conceding, however, that Leonardo may have added "a few touches" to "brighten" up the little panel.[15]

He surmises that Credi painted this masterpiece at the time that Leonardo was engaged upon the "Adoration of the Magi," that is to say in the years 1481–82, when we know the younger artist was twenty-one or twenty-two years of age. Now this is just about the time that Credi's mother made the Fiscal Declaration to which we have already referred. We learn from it, as we have already stated, that the young Credi and his mother were living in great poverty, and that as a *garzone* in Verrocchio's studio the son received an incredibly small wage. Allowing for a certain element of exaggeration that is often to be found in such declarations, we can still say with Müntz, "Il n'était guère possible de vivre dans des conditions plus modestes!"[16]

It is really unnecessary, at this time of day, to argue that the predella panels could not have been painted in 1481 or 1482; as we now know that for "more than six years" before November, 1485, the work on the great altarpiece had been suspended and that the executors of Bishop Donato had stopped the payment of instalments due for it. The fact is that at the time the "Madonna di Piazza" was being completed—that is to say in 1485 and 1486—Leonardo was actually residing in Milan; and we have no record of the artist's being in Tuscany in those years.

It must be conceded that the "Madonna di Piazza" as we see it today, although it is a composite work, has a certain obvious unity. And it is this unity that has led a few critics to declare it to be the sole work of one master, against the evidence of documents, and against all probability, when we take into account the working of the great studio from which it emanated.

[15] That Leonardo, whose somber color schemes are well known, should, in his early *sfumato* period, have taken upon himself to "brighten up" a picture seems to me a somewhat surprising suggestion.

[16] E. Müntz, "Les Déclarations de Bien ... de Lorenzo di Credi," *Chronique des Arts* (Paris, 1899), p. 312.

What is the nature of this unity? It is twofold: It is in part organic and in part superficial. It is organic because Verrocchio created such a well-balanced, well-articulated monumental design, a design that owes much, as we have said, to Verrocchio's master, Alesso Baldovinetti. For whatever failings Baldovinetti had as an artist, he was a master of composition in the grand manner.

The picture's superficial appearance of unity is due to Credi. As we scan it more closely, "we perceive, here and there," as I pointed out several years ago, "the existence of a *velatura;* which produces the same kind of effect that we find in the work of an old master, of which some parts have been glazed over by some slick, impious restorer of to-day, who fondly imagined that he was improving the picture."[17]

Sir Kenneth Clark, writing more recently,[18] expresses a similar opinion of Credi's work on the "Madonna di Piazza." But he certainly exaggerates when he says that "every inch of it shows Credi's smug, lifeless handling."

The altarpiece was nearly finished when Credi got to work on it; and, like a restorer, he began to fill up the holes in it. But, as incompetent restorers have so often discovered, he soon realized that what he had painted did not match well the surrounding color. He, therefore, extended the area of his repaints, in his efforts to create a superficial harmony.[19]

For example, Credi painted over entirely the figures of the Madonna and the Child. He also glazed over the figure of St. John the Baptist, so admirably conceived by his master. The figure of S. Donato has suffered less. It is this figure that, on further study, I believe to have been painted, at least in great part, by Leonardo, after Verrocchio's original design. It is quite impossible that Credi could have conceived or executed so noble a figure. To Verrocchio, it owes its statuesque quality; to Leonardo, the admirable painting of the drapery, and, above all, the V-shaped folds, upon the ground, of the long alb. These

[17] R. Langton Douglas, *Leonardo da Vinci—His San Donato and the Tax Collector*, p. 31.

[18] *Leonardo da Vinci* (New York and Cambridge, England, 1939), p. 26.

[19] Douglas, *op. cit.*, p. 31.

clean-cut folds we see in that part of the Uffizi "Baptism" that was painted by him, in the Munich "Madonna," and in the "Annunciation" of the Louvre. The folds that he paints are as far removed as possible from the rounded, flannel-like folds that we see in all of Credi's authentic works. For the rest, Credi glazed over parts of the background, with the object of securing the desired unity of effect. But how little, in reality, the altarpiece owes to Credi, becomes manifest when we look at that artist's pictures.

Fortunately, the predella suffered less from Credi's disfigurements than did the rest of the altarpiece.[20] In the "Annunciation" we find hardly a trace of Credi's hand. In the "San Donato and the Tax Collector" he seems to have repainted the head of Eustatius, the tax collector, and some part of his figure. In fact, the head of this man is almost pure Credi. But the lower part of the cloak that lies upon the ground owes nothing to that artist. Here we find once more the same V-shaped folds that are to be seen in Leonardo's other early pictures and drawings. When Berenson surmises that the predella was painted by Credi and then touched up, in parts, by Leonardo, he puts the cart before the horse. Two panels of the predella were certainly designed by Leonardo and, in great part, finished by him. Unfortunately, on one of the panels, Credi added a few final touches. There are, however, in this little panel, certain details which are even more characteristic of Leonardo than anything in the "Annunciation." In his *Trattato della Pittura*, Leonardo stresses the importance of giving to each figure its proper gesture. The drawing of the right hand of Eustatius with its pointing forefinger is peculiarly characteristic of Leonardo. We find it in such works of his as the "Virgin of the Rocks," the "Last Supper," the "Madonna with the Yarn-Winder," the "St. John the Baptist," and also in the "Bacchus" of the Louvre, which was painted after his design. Moreover, in this little picture, as I have already pointed out, we see, in the morse that fastens the Bishop's cope, a jewel similar to that in the Dreyfus "Madonna" and

[20] The drawing in the Galleria Corsini in Rome, "Studio di Panneggiamento," is, I believe, a study for the Virgin in the Louvre "Annunciation" (see Enrico Bodmer, *Disegni di Leonardo* [Florence: Sansoni, 1939], Pl. 44 and p. 20).

closely resembling the clasp of the Virgin's cloak in the Benois
"Madonna," the Munich "Madonna," and the "Virgin of the
Rocks." In the background, too, of the picture, we find trees
that are cut off at the top, in just the same way as is the large
tree in the "Adoration of the Magi" at the Uffizi, one of the
few generally accepted works of Leonardo's early period. It
would be possible to indicate other details of drawing that are
characteristic of Leonardo; but those that I have given are
sufficient for my purpose.

Berenson admits that he finds in the "Annunciation" the tone
of Leonardo, and not that of Credi, and that the landscape of
this picture is also not by Credi.[21] The truth is that the color
of the "Annunciation" and the San Donato panel, like the
drawing, is peculiarly characteristic of Leonardo, and quite different from the crude, garish color schemes that we find in
Lorenzo di Credi's pictures.[22] The landscape, too, in the two
little panels is clearly by the master's own hand.

In these works we see only a slight appearance of *sfumato*, for
Leonardo's *sfumato* period was only just beginning. We see this
new style of his gradually developing in such works as the
Benois "Madonna." In the two predella panels, however, we
find already the golden brown and reddish color harmonies that
we are to see later in the "Virgin of the Rocks."

All this evidence tends to prove that Morelli was right when
he maintained that the "Madonna di Piazza" altarpiece was a
work of Verrocchio, and when he further concluded that the
panel of the "Annunciation" (which we now know formed a
part of its predella) was the work of Leonardo. The "San
Donato and the Tax Collector," even though it has suffered a
little from Credi's attentions, must also be attributed to
Leonardo.

[21] *The Drawings of the Florentine Painters of the Renaissance* (Chicago, 1938), I, 59: "Moreover, the
trees and the landscape have nothing of Credi, nor the tone either. Both landscape and tone seem
as much Leonardo's as other elements seem Credi's."

[22] The color scheme of the panel at Worcester is even further removed from the color schemes
of Credi than is that of the "Annunciation." This fact I must again point out, as some critics
who have not seen this little picture, or who have but a passing acquaintance with it, seem to be
unaware of it.

CHAPTER VIII

LEONARDO'S PICTURES
THE SECOND FLORENTINE PERIOD

THE year 1478 proved, as we have said, to be the turning-point of Leonardo's life. In January of that year he received an important, independent commission—a commission from the Government of the Republic. And we know, from an inscription in Leonardo's own handwriting on a drawing in the Uffizi, that, in the following autumn, he was at work on two Madonnas. It is generally agreed that one of these pictures was the Benois "Madonna."

The altarpiece that Leonardo agreed to make for the Signory of Florence, as we have already noted, was never finished. The earliest of the pictures known to us which the young artist painted when he set out to work on his own account is the "Madonna and Child" now at Leningrad. This picture clearly reveals that, for Leonardo, the days of tutelage and imitation were over. No longer, in designing a painting, would he make use of some drawing by his master: He would make his own drawings for any picture that he planned to create. He had, in fact, started on an entirely new path. A period of accelerated development had begun for him, a period which was to reach its culmination in the creation of that masterpiece of the High Renaissance, the "Adoration of the Magi."

The "Madonna and Child" of Munich, painted, as we believe, but a short time before the Benois "Madonna," was, notwithstanding certain details that indicate to us the gradual evolution of Leonardo's personal style, a work of the school of Verrocchio. The Benois "Madonna" is an entirely original work. It reveals to us that, at the age of twenty-six, the young artist had broken with his past.

His first steps it must be admitted are a little faltering. The Benois "Madonna" is not a great picture. It has certain obvious faults as a work of art, and is, perhaps, a little repulsive as an illustration. But it is entirely original in its conception. It does not rely, for the composition of the figures, on any design by another artist. Leonardo himself made drawings for it, of which the best of those that survive is that which is in the Louvre. These brilliant sketches are entirely spontaneous and personal in style, and are full of life and movement. With a swift, sensitive line, the artist records his vision; and the force and fire of the creative impulse had but little diminished when he painted his picture.

I cannot agree with those who hold that the painting itself is greatly inferior in vigor to the drawings that he made when he began the work. I think that, in arriving at such a conclusion, they allowed themselves to be swayed by emotions that are not in themselves artistic—emotions similar, in fact, to those that dominated Berenson when, in his later years, he contemplated the "Monna Lisa." They did not like the woman that Leonardo had taken for a model; and they liked still less the child. There is, it is true, but little charm in Leonardo's representation of the Virgin; and the infant that he painted is almost a monster; but the little picture is full of life, and in it Leonardo expresses simply and sincerely his own feelings regarding the one normal human relationship about which he felt very deeply—the relation of the mother and the child. The picture now at the Hermitage is admittedly inferior in quality to the drawing at the Louvre; but it is, nevertheless, a sincere and moving expression of the artist's deepest feelings.

Leonardo's development throughout the three years that followed his visit to Pistoia was extraordinarily rapid. It was in these years that he made a series of remarkable drawings for a picture of which the subject was the "Adoration of the Shepherds." It is quite possible that this was the subject which he finally chose for the altarpiece that he had agreed to execute for the Chapel of the Signoria. But this picture was never finished.[1] And, in March, 1481, Leonardo undertook to paint, for the

[1] Kenneth Clark, "Adoration of the Shepherds and Dragon Fight," *Burlington Magazine*, 1933, pp. 21–26.

monks of S. Donato a Scopeto, a picture with a kindred subject, an "Adoration of the Kings."

In all probability, it was in the year 1481 that he made that beautiful design which is now in the Louvre, the Gallichon drawing. We learn from it that Leonardo's first idea for the altarpiece was to place the scene amongst the ruins of an old Roman palace, a palace with an imposing staircase. The New Life coming into being, amidst the wreckage of the Old Order! Later on he changed the composition. This very dramatic artist began to realize that the huge staircase was rather a cumbersome old stage-property. He moves the Virgin and Child and the crowd of attendant figures into the open air, and the Madonna is now represented seated in the shade of a tall oak tree. But the Roman palace with its huge staircase is still retained. It is now a prominent feature in the background of the picture.

In some ways the unfinished picture at the Uffizi is inferior to the original drawing at the Louvre. It has many more figures; it is more vividly imagined; it has a richer scheme of chiaroscuro; but, great work as it is, it has less unity, is less harmonious, less rhythmical. In some respects, it is true, it is far more dramatic; but it is less spontaneous, less entirely expressive of that sincerity of feeling which is essential to a great religious picture.

It has, too, great as it undoubtedly is, another obvious fault. In a picture, as in a stage play—a great tragedy, for example— the background should not be obtrusive. It must not attract the eye or draw away the attention of the spectator for a moment from the momentous scene that is being enacted. In this respect the picture is thoroughly Florentine in character. It gives those who are not really interested in the art of painting, and who are not deeply affected by a great picture, something to occupy their minds.

The scene of the "Adoration of the Kings" is vividly imagined. The main part of the picture—that is to say the whole of the foreground—has a well-defined pattern, and is admirably composed. The center of it has the form of an isosceles triangle surmounted by an arc. The apex of the triangle is very near the Virgin's head. On either side of the central group, on the extreme right and the extreme left of it, there is a vertical, calm, erect figure. These two figures—one of them an old man, a philosopher, representing the life of thought; the other a young man, full of vigor, representing the life of action—like the wings on a stage, help to contain and to frame the swaying sea of eager, agitated worshipers. The picture is full of emotion, vividly realized. But there are disturbing elements in its too restless, crowded setting. A considerable part of the background is made up of traditional lumber, iconographically obscure and artistically superfluous. It distracts the onlooker, it leads him to ask questions, when his thoughts and feelings should be fully engaged by the main theme.

The huge oak tree, too, cut off at the top, which is in the middle distance, is too large, too prominent. It tends to dwarf the principal figure, and to lead the eye upward away from the Virgin and the Child to the contemplation of a meaningless, truncated mass of foliage.

The most obtrusive of all the details in the background is, of course, the great palace staircase. The monotony of its endless flight of stairs—all of which, naturally, are of a similar size and shape—recalls to the modern man the tedious feeling that he experienced when he first gazed at the endless rows of windows —windows of precisely the same size and shape—in a lofty New York edifice of today.

This staircase of a ruined Roman palace is not an invention of Leonardo. We find it, for example, but in a less prominent position in Fra Filippo Lippi's early "Nativity" in the Uffizi.[2] Why did Leonardo give it such a conspicuous position in his designs for the picture? What is its justification? He spatch-cocked it most awkwardly into the otherwise harmonious, lovely composition of the Gallichon drawing. Leonardo feels that it is out of place; but he has not the courage to get rid of it, to throw out of doors this unwieldy foster-child of his constructive imagination. He, therefore, moves it into the background on the other side of the picture. From which we conclude that too great a regard for iconological tradition may prove as great a stumbling-block to a painter as too great an addiction to scientific study. If an artist allows himself to be

[2] No. 8350.

swayed by some branch of archaeological or scientific study to the detriment of his art, "the hungry sheep look up and are not fed" with life-enhancing emotions, as they contemplate his works. They are in fact "swollen with wind, and the rank mist they draw."

How human all this is! What a common experience it is—not only with the painter of pictures, but with the poet, the writer of prose, the musical composer, and perhaps even more with the interior decorator and the strategist. Suddenly a man is called upon to slay the offspring of his imagination or his mind. Something that he once cherished has to go, because he realizes that it is out of place and threatens to mar the whole work that he had in hand. When a creative worker feels tempted to retain such an excrescence he must act promptly and ruthlessly. He must "cut it off, and cast it from him." Leonardo, it seems, had not the courage to do this. He was dissatisfied with his work: He knew what was wrong; but he temporized. For this spoiled child of fortune could not face the labor involved, first of all, in changing the background of his composition, and then in setting quietly to work to finish the whole picture. He put off a decision. Finally he shut the doors of his studio and stole away. He was soon on the road to Milan.

But he left behind him a work that, with all its faults, is one of the world's great masterpieces, a picture that haunts the imagination when the memory of many great, impeccable works begins to fade. We can never forget the serene figure of the Virgin, nor the swaying, eager throng of prophets, seers, and wise men, their eyes fixed on the glowing vision, long dreamed of, long foretold—the heavenly vision of the incarnate Son of God. "The Word was made flesh, and dwelt among us. And we ourselves beheld his glory, the glory of the only begotten Son of the Father, full of grace and truth."

There are two other pictures that belong to this period of accelerated transition, that were executed shortly before Leonardo left Florence for Milan, the "St. Jerome" of the Vatican and the Litta "Madonna" at Leningrad. Neither of these pictures is of any great artistic importance. Moreover, one of them—the "St. Jerome"—which has had a sad history, is in a very bad state of preservation. The other, the Litta "Madonna" was finished by a pupil, and, in later times, has been entirely repainted. How beautiful the head of the Madonna must have been we can realize when we look at the drawing for it in the Louvre. The "St. Jerome," a realistic study of a nude old man, with a background of rock, clearly belongs to the same period as the "Adoration of the Magi." We find in it a similar treatment of chiaroscuro; and the head of St. Jerome closely resembles the head of an old man in the larger composition.

The Litta "Madonna" seems to be the same picture that is mentioned in a list of Leonardo's drawings and paintings in the *Codice Atlantico*,[3] which, judging from internal evidence, belongs to the year 1482. It is, perhaps, a list of the drawings and paintings that Leonardo took with him to Milan in that year. In it we find mention of two Madonnas, "una nostra Donna finjta, un altra quasi che in proffilo." The first of these two Madonnas cannot be identified, and the second was, in all probability, the Litta "Madonna." The third item in the same list reads "certi san girolamj." This item probably consisted of drawings for the picture of "St. Jerome" which Leonardo had recently painted.

The last work that belongs to this second Florentine period is a picture that was actually painted in Milan, soon after Leonardo's arrival in that city, the "Virgin of the Rocks." Leonardo, as we have already stated, received the commission for this picture in April, 1482. But not only does it belong to Leonardo's second Florentine period: it is even a little *retardataire* in style. That is to say, it is not so clearly a work of the High Renaissance as the "Adoration of the Magi." The growing plants in the foreground recall the Uffizi "Adoration." The background of fantastic rocks reminds us of other Florentine paintings—of works of Botticini, of early works of Piero di Cosimo. Whilst the Madonna, spreading her protecting cloak over poor humanity, as represented by the infant St. John, recalls several Sienese paintings of Our Lady of Pity, of an earlier date. A drawing of Leonardo in the Metropolitan Museum was

---

[3] *Codice Atlantico*, 324ʳ. See Kenneth Clark, "The Madonna in Profile," *Burlington Magazine*, 1933, pp. 136–40.

inspired by the main theme of this picture—the blessed Virgin protecting the infant Precursor, and blessing and safeguarding her little Son.

This picture shows us that those are entirely mistaken who say that Leonardo had not any normal feelings in regard to woman and her function in the world. No picture of any age has more fully, more tenderly expressed a mother's love of children, a mother's solicitude for them, a mother's protecting care. "As a hen gathers her chickens under her wings," so the Blessed Virgin endeavors to guard her own little Son and the infant St. John against all dangers. Whilst the child Jesus gives his blessing to his forerunner, the Angel, seated near him on the ground, points to St. John as one of the first of mankind to recognize the divinity of Jesus, and to kneel before Him with his tiny hands joined in supplication. How carefully has Leonardo drawn all the expressive hands in this picture—the right hand of Christ, both of the hands of his Mother, the right hand of St. John, the hand of the Angel. To this picture alone, of all his important pictures, he had the patience to give completely that careful finish which his own artistic principles demanded in a painting. Even the "Last Supper" and the portrait of "La Gioconda" were not quite finished.

Unfortunately, this work appears to be more *sfumato* in character than it really is. We cannot fully enjoy the subtle, delicate modeling, the pure flesh tones of the faces and the hands of these four young figures, nor the bright colors of the flowers and foliage, and the early morning sky; for this picture, like the Benois "Madonna" and the "Monna Lisa," is covered with thick coatings of dirt and old varnish. Some day, perhaps, in a happier world, a great restorer will be found, conscientious and full of reverence, and at the same time richly endowed with artistic knowledge and experience, who will be possessed of an unswerving desire to show his fellow-men as much as possible of the original handiwork of this great master, and to reveal to them the pure color tones and sensitive gradations of light and shade that are now seen "as through a glass darkly"—a glass of dusky amber tone that robs a masterpiece of much of its quality and charm.

CHAPTER IX

LEONARDO'S PICTURES
THE FIRST MILANESE PERIOD. I
THE PORTRAITS

IT IS now clear, from evidence derived from the letters and other writings of Leonardo's contemporaries, that this painter, in his two periods of residence in Milan, made more pictures than some art critics have imagined. It is true that Sabba da Castiglione and Fra Pietro da Novellara, writing in the sixteenth century, deplore that Leonardo was absorbed in geometry and that he gave little time to painting; but there is plenty of evidence to show that, after these periods of comparative neglect of his vocation, the artist returned again and again, if only for brief periods, to his first and greatest love, the art of painting. We have already spoken about his "little Madonnas." We know that during the long period of his employment by Lodovico il Moro, he also painted several portraits, some of which were finished by assistants. We are told, for example, that he made portraits of two of Lodovico's mistresses, Cecilia Gallerani and Lucrezia Crivelli. The portrait of Lucrezia cannot now be identified: That of Cecilia Gallerani was, at the beginning of the second World War, in the gallery at Cracow. That this portrait does represent Cecilia Gallerani is proved by the fact that the artist has chosen to paint her nursing an animal of the weasel tribe, an ermine. For the Greek word for ermine is γαλέη, and Lodovico, perhaps because of his love for Cecilia, sometimes used a representation of an ermine as his own badge.

Leonardo, as we know from a letter that Cecilia wrote to Isabella d'Este, painted her when she was very young. It is probable, therefore, that this picture was commissioned soon after Cecilia became Lodovico's mistress, that is to say, in the

year 1482. That it was executed in the season of winter is clear
from the fact that the ermine's fur is pure white and not brown.
It is, therefore, reasonable to conclude that this picture was
painted soon after Leonardo's arrival in the city, in the winter
of 1482–83 or in the following winter.

To me it seems that the ermine dominates the composition and
that the portrait ought to bear the title "An Ermine Held by a
Young Lady." But that was not the impression that the picture
made on Bellincioni, a contemporary poet, who composed some
verses, in dialogue form, entitled "Sopra il Ritracto di Madona
Cicilia qual Fece Maestro Leonardo."[1] Bellincioni clearly
thought Cecilia the star of the piece; for he writes:

"POETA: Di che t'adiri? A chi invidia hai natura?
NATURA: Al Vinci che ha ritratto una tua stella;
            Cecilia si bellisima hoggi è quella
            Che a' suoi begli occhi el sol par umbra oscura. . . . ."

In the whole poem, there is not a word about the ermine.

I am not qualified to write dogmatically about the authorship
of this portrait, as I have not seen the picture itself. But the
most authoritative of modern critics of Italian painting are
agreed that it is a work of Leonardo.[2]

There are grounds for believing that Leonardo received commissions for male portraits; but only one of them has survived,
the "Portrait of a Musician" at the Ambrosiana. The treatment
of the hair is very characteristic of Leonardo, as also is the
delicate modeling of the young man's face. Fortunately, we are
able to enjoy fully the fine quality of this work; for, unlike
almost all of Leonardo's other paintings, it is clean and well-
preserved. But, pleasing as this portrait is, it is not an epoch-
making picture, and it tells us but little about its subject. In
view of Leonardo's personal history, it is a strange psycho-
logical fact that, in this portrait as in the representations of
men in his large compositions, Leonardo does not show such

[1] L. Beltrami, *Documenti e Memorie riguardanti la Vita e le Opere di Leonardo da Vinci* (Milan,
1919), p. 207.

[2] B. Berenson, *Pitture Italiane del Rinascimento* (Milan, 1936), p. 239; A. Venturi, *Storia dell'Arte
Italiana* (Milan, 1925), IX, 100–103.

revealing insight as he does when he paints women. Even his caricatures of men are, for the most part, a little superficial, a little obvious. Leonardo, in fact, from his early years, both in his drawings and in his paintings, reveals a remarkable, intuitive understanding of women—girls, wives, and mothers—an understanding that owes its origin to sympathy. Was he not throughout his life, owing to some mischance of his youth, a frustrated, homesick wanderer?

In view of the fact that Leonardo was employed continuously, for so long a time, by Lodovico il Moro, and received commissions to paint persons connected with his Court, it would have been strange if the great master had not been asked to make portraits of the Duke and his consort, after Lodovico's marriage to Beatrice d'Este. For Leonardo was the Court Painter. He was the Duke's guest at his castle of Vigevano, on at least two occasions, spending some time with the newly married pair at this, their true home. We know, of course, that after the death of Beatrice he did paint portraits, in fresco, of the Duke and Duchess in the foreground of Montorfano's "Crucifixion" at Santa Maria delle Grazie—portraits that are now obliterated. But it is impossible to believe that Leonardo was not commissioned by his host to portray the young wife that Lodovico loved so much, when he was living under their roof, in the years 1492 and 1494.

In the last generation, some writers on Leonardo maintained that there was no portrait of Beatrice d'Este by Leonardo's hand in Milan a year after her death, and that Leonardo had never painted the Duchess, except on the walls of the Refectory of Santa Maria delle Grazie.[3] But the reasons given for this conclusion are altogether inadequate. It is argued that Isabella d'Este, when, in the year 1498, she wished to see an example of Leonardo's work, would not have asked Cecilia Gallerani for a loan of Leonardo's picture of her, had there been in Milan a portrait of Beatrice d'Este by Leonardo. McCurdy, and those writers who are in agreement with him, overlook the fact that

[3] E. McCurdy, *Leonardo da Vinci* (London: George Bell & Sons, 1904), p. 40; and Julia Cartwright, *Beatrice d'Este* (London, 1899), p. 91.

there were two excellent reasons why Isabella did not approach
Lodovico with a request for the loan of his wife's portrait. In
the first place, the relations then existing between the courts
of Milan and Mantua were far from cordial. Lodovico suspected, and with good reason, that his brother-in-law, the
Marchese, was by no means a loyal friend of his and that he was
about to give assistance to those powers that were bent on his
ruin. Isabella, it is true, had continued to correspond with the
Duke; but it was unlikely that, at that moment, she would have
asked so great a favor of him. For she must have known that her
request would be refused. She was fully aware that Lodovico
had never ceased to mourn the loss of Beatrice, going every day
to Santa Maria delle Grazie to assist at Masses for the repose of
her soul. The truth is that the Duke, though he had been by no
means a perfect husband, was always sincerely and passionately
devoted to his young wife. Let us not deceive ourselves. Do we
not know full well that, in a society where polygamy has never
been, in actual fact, a very uncommon phenomenon, Lodovico
was a lover of no very rare type? And, since Remorse is the parent
of Fidelity, Lodovico would have been very reluctant to part
with the portrait of his dead wife.

To maintain, as some do, that the Duchess would not have
employed Leonardo because he had painted her husband's
former mistress is an argument that is contradicted by the facts.
For Beatrice actually did employ Leonardo at Vigevano, and he
stayed there as her honored guest.

In a previous chapter, we have given good reasons for believing that in Leonardo's collection there were two cartoons of
the Duchess that were attributed to him, and that were subsequently in the heritage of Francesco Melzi.[4] We believe that
the Castel-Pizzuto portrait of Beatrice d'Este was painted at
Vigevano[5] and that it is the picture of her to which her cousin
Niccolò da Correggio, the court poet, refers in a sonnet com-

---

[4] E. Wright, *Some Observations Made in Travelling through France and Italy . . . . in the Years 1720
and 1722* (London, 1730), p. 471 (see chap. iv).

[5] There is a version of this portrait in the Musée André in Paris by some imitator of Leonardo,
probably Bernardino de' Conti.

posed in her honor at the time of her early death.[6] Having
agreed to make a picture of so intelligent and so imperious a
lady, the wife of his chief patron, Leonardo would not, we
think, have dared to hand over the execution of it to a pupil; as
we know that he was accustomed to do in the case of portraits
of lesser personages that he had been commissioned to paint.

The best authenticated portraits of the Duchess are: (1) the
copper proof of a Milanese coin of 1495; (2) the marble bust of
Gian Cristoforo Romano in the Louvre, executed before 1491;
(3) the portrait of Beatrice in the Pala Sforzesca in the Brera
Gallery, finished in 1495, which some authorities attribute to
Bernardino de' Conti; (4) the miniature portrait of Beatrice
d'Este on an Act of Donation, wrongly attributed to Fra Antonio da Monza, which is in the British Museum;[7] and (5) the
sculptured effigy on the sarcophagus by Cristoforo Solari in the
Certosa at Pavia. All these representations of Beatrice d'Este are
of the character of portraits of ceremony. They represent the
Duchess as she appeared at some court function, when appareled
in one of those magnificent dresses which she loved. But none of
the writers on the Castel-Pizzuto portrait have referred to two
other contemporary portraits in which she is represented, with
her hair loose, in the kind of dress that she would wear in her
own home; (6) her profile portrait, which is in the Castello
Sforzesco at Milan[8]—a copy of a lost original; and (7) the
representation of the Duchess, painted after her early death,
that is to be found on the frescoed ceiling of the palace of
Lodovico il Moro in Ferrara—a palace which was begun for

[6] Suida has discussed this portrait in a recent article entitled "A Leonardo Profile and Dynamism in Portraiture" (*Art in America*, April, 1941, pp. 62 ff.); see also G. M. Richter in *Art in
America* (July, 1941), "A Leonardo Profile."

An article on portraits of Beatrice d'Este by Valentiner was published in *Art in America* in
January, 1937. Valentiner holds that "it is more than likely that Lodovico had a portrait of his
wife painted by Leonardo during her lifetime, as he had a genuine love for her." But we are
unable to agree with him that the so-called "La Belle Ferronière" is that portrait.

Giorgio Nicodemi, director of the Castello Sforzesco Museum, holds that the Castel-Pizzuto
portrait of Beatrice d'Este by Leonardo is identical with a portrait of the Duchess which, a
century ago, was in the possession of a monk of the Certosa di Pavia, Count Frisiani.

[7] Reproduced in G. Clausse, *Les Sforza et les Arts au Milanais* (Paris, 1909), Pl. XXXIV, p. 495.

[8] See O. Sirén, *Leonardo da Vinci, the Artist and the Man* (London and New Haven: Yale University Press, 1916), p. 58.

him, as a refuge, by his friend Costabili, the ambassador at the
Court of Milan, when the fall of the ill-fated Duke was near at
hand.

Without doubt, there were in existence at that time several
portraits—both drawings and paintings—of Isabella d'Este and
her sister. Such portraits were made use of by some unknown
Ferrarese imitator of Mantegna, when, at the beginning of the
sixteenth century, he depicted the two young princesses in a
fresco in Lodovico's palace, in the building that was left unfinished, after it had become certain that the Duke was to be
detained as a prisoner by the King of France.[9]

We know that Beatrice, like her sister, must often have been
represented in paintings that were not portraits of ceremony.
But the likeness of her in Lodovico's palace in Ferrara is especially important in view of the surprising fact that some
writers on the Castel-Pizzuto portrait[10] consider it "a strong
argument" against the identification of its subject with Beatrice
d'Este that, in this picture, the lady is not wearing a magnificent
court dress, covered with jewels, nor is her abundant hair
braided! It is certain that, as a king does not wear his crown
when he goes to bed, so Beatrice, fond of dress though she was,
did not always array herself as though she were about to attend
a court function. Like her sister (who also loved fine clothes)
and her niece, Leonora, she was sometimes painted in the
ordinary costume worn by a lady of high position when she
was in her own home.

In the frescoed portrait at Ferrara, Beatrice, as was natural,
was given the greater prominence. "She can be at once recognized," says Luzio, "because of the very evident resemblance
of the head of the young figure on the right to the bust of
Beatrice in the Louvre by Gian Cristoforo Romano." The two
sisters are represented as they might have been dressed on some

---

[9] The chief authority on the iconography of Isabella d'Este and her sister Beatrice is Alessandro
Luzio. Luzio has discovered many important documents relating to the two sisters. In one of his
books, *La Galleria Gonzaga*, he discusses fully the portraits of these princesses and makes special
mention of these representations of them at Ferrara, as they were in the heyday of their youth
(pp. 187, 188, and Pl. at p. 32).

[10] W. Suida, *op. cit.*, p. 67.

summer morning when they looked down from the balcony of
the music-room of some great palace. They have loose, flowing
hair and are without any jewels, save for a fine, slender chain.

Those who find it difficult to believe that a great lady would
refuse to be painted in any other costume but court attire can
have but little knowledge of the practice of great portrait
painters, and of their methods of work. And it is not only the
great masters who are accustomed to decide for themselves how
a sitter should be painted. Any competent artist who "sees his
portrait" insists on painting his own vision of his subject.
Those who frequent the society of living painters know of many
cases of this kind. Is it not probable, therefore, that the master-
ful Leonardo, who had dared more than once to snub that
great lady, Isabella d'Este, would insist on painting her sister,
the Duchess, *as he himself saw her*, at a time when he was staying
with the ducal pair in their castle of Vigevano? Is it not
probable, too, that her husband wished to have her painted as
she appeared in ordinary life, in their home in the country?

The Castel-Pizzuto picture, in its details of dress, resembles
many portraits of princesses of the house of Este. We recall, for
example, the portrait of Isabella at the Louvre, attributed by
Luzio to Costa, and by Berenson to Bartolommeo Veneto; the
portraits of Leonora d'Este at Hampton Court and in the Bache
Collection; and the representation of Isabella and her daughter
Leonora that is to be found in that picture in the Louvre that
is called "La Cour d'Isabella d'Este"; and also the portrait of
Isabella and Beatrice in the fresco at Ferrara, to which we have
just referred. In all of these portraits, we see the sitter's hair
hanging loose, without any band to confine it, or with only a
slender chain encircling the head near the top of the forehead.[11]
In all of them the ladies wear but one other piece of jewelry, a
fine chain around the neck. In all of them, too, the chemise is
visible, where the dress is slashed at the shoulders. In the
Castel-Pizzuto portrait, we find the same features as we see in
other contemporary portraits of Beatrice—the strongly marked,
deep line where her nose meets her cheek, the small full mouth,

[11] See Appendix VI.

and the round chin. Above all, we find in this portrait the very characteristic heavy mass of hair that falls loosely in waves,[12] just as it does in the portrait of the young Beatrice in the fresco at Ferrara, and in the portrait at the Castello Sforzesco. We realize, too, as we look at this picture, that it was painted at the time when her sister reported that the Duchess was already growing fat, "like Madonna her mother." We do not think, then, that it is possible to escape the conclusion that the Castel-Pizzuto picture is a portrait of Beatrice d'Este.

Having decided whom this portrait represents, we shall proceed to show who was its author. The portraits attributed to Leonardo that are now generally accepted as works of his are few in number; and they contain but few morphological details that can help us to determine the authorship of the Castel-Pizzuto picture. In one important detail, however, we observe at once the unmistakable handiwork of the master, the living vital hair that is so entirely characteristic of the author of "La Gioconda." The master's chief imitators, Bernardino de' Conti and Ambrogio de Predis, never painted hair like this.

As regards its color, this portrait has, at present, one great advantage over all Leonardo's other pictures, except the portrait of "Ginevra dei Benci" and "The Musician." It is possible to find in it those "infinitely minute gradations of light" that are the essence of the *sfumato* style—gradations that it is quite impossible to see in some of the master's greatest works, owing to the fact that they are covered with a brown film of dirt and old varnish that conceals their true quality. It is owing to the fact that a thick patina covers such pictures as the "Monna Lisa" and the "Adoration of the Magi" that most people have altogether wrong ideas about Leonardo's *sfumato* manner.

The fine quality of the "Beatrice d'Este" leads us to the conclusion that none of Leonardo's pupils and the imitators could have painted it. It could not have been the work of either of those followers of his to whom we have just referred, Bernardino de' Conti and Ambrogio de Predis, whose names have

[12] B. Berenson, "Verrocchio e Leonardo," *Bollettino d'Arte*, December, 1933, p. 360; and in his *The Drawings of the Florentine Painters of the Renaissance* (Chicago, 1938), I, 66.

been put forward by some contemporary writers on the subject as its possible author. The later replica of this picture, which is in the Musée Jacquemart-André in Paris, has been given by Berenson to Bernardino de' Conti, an artist who, in his own heavy-handed style, imitated his master to the best of his ability. At the same time, Berenson admits that the Castel-Pizzuto portrait is certainly of finer quality than its replica in Paris. The truth is that Bernardino never produced work of this high standard of excellence. Neither did Ambrogio de Predis, that rather dull painter of profile portraits. Only once or twice, when under his master's direct inspiration, did Ambrogio succeed in making a really fine picture; but never did he create a work of such quality as this.

Above all, in the *composition* of this painting, we find the hand of Leonardo. From the first, he visualized his whole design in a connected rhythm, in which the eye is led away from the foremost plane of the picture. This was his object in his earliest-known work, that is to say in that portion of the "Baptism" of Verrocchio, which is from his hand. To create an illusion of space, to give his figures form and movement, to give depth to the composition—these were his aims. It is significant that he once advised a pupil to study Donatello, to go back to the fountain-head of the Florentine Renaissance, and not to imitate those who had modified and prettified the style of the great leader.

It is one of the most remarkable facts in art history that few of his Milanese followers seem to have realized this aim of their master, who, in 1481, in his "Adoration of the Magi"—that astounding composition!—had given the keynote to the High Renaissance. For the type of portrait that they most favored was the profile portrait. Even Ambrogio de Predis, who, next to Boltraffio, was Leonardo's chief assistant, shows but little sympathy with his master's aims. In how few unaided works of his own composition do we find any resolute attempt to see figures in the round, to render significant form, and space, and movement, as did the creator of this "Portrait of Beatrice d'Este."

In this picture, as in some of Leonardo's contemporary drawings,[13] his aim is clearly quite different from that of the painters
of the flat, static figures in so many Milanese portraits. The
well-rounded form of its subject is rendered with infinite subtlety. No photograph can do justice to the delicate, sensitive
modeling of the neck and bust of the Duchess—modeling which
is cunningly assisted by the significant line of the slender chain
that Beatrice wears. Here, as in the whole unified, rhythmical
composition of this portrait, we find the handiwork of Leonardo
da Vinci.

Before concluding this chapter on the portraits painted by
Leonardo during his long residence in northern Italy, I would
like to add a few words on the subject of the cartoon of Isabella
d'Este that is in the Louvre. This cartoon has been generally
regarded by writers on Leonardo as one of the two cartoons that
Leonardo made of the Marchioness, when at Mantua. The
writer, however, of the most recent authoritative work on
Leonardo is of the opinion that it is not the original cartoon
because, in it, the right arm is "in a position anatomically
false." At the same time, he accepts as an original work
Leonardo's red-chalk drawing for the "Last Supper" in the
Venice Academy, whilst admitting that it is "badly drawn,"
and that "the Christ's right arm and hand are childish."[14] The
fact is that even Leonardo sometimes drew badly and that the
original defects of the Isabella d'Este portrait have probably
been accentuated by injuries and maladroit restorations. All
cartoons of this type have suffered from ill usage. This cartoon,
notwithstanding its defects, has the indefinable quality of the
master's authentic works. It has a certain distinction that is entirely wanting in the works of Leonardo's followers in Milan,
from which city this drawing originally came. From what we
know of its history, it is reasonable to conclude that it was one
of the collection of cartoons which formed a part of the heritage
of Francesco Melzi.

[13] For example, Windsor, No. 12.513. This drawing, I believe, belongs to Leonardo's first
Milanese period.

[14] Kenneth Clark, *Leonardo da Vinci* (Cambridge, England, 1939), pp. 105 and 97.

CHAPTER X

LEONARDO'S PICTURES

THE FIRST MILANESE PERIOD. II
THE LAST SUPPER

I CAN clearly recall the moment when, as a young man, I first caught sight of Leonardo's "Last Supper." I had entered the Convent of Santa Maria delle Grazie in the hope of receiving a great experience. I had, of course, seen many reproductions of the "Last Supper"; but I had never placed much faith in the evidence that a reproduction affords as to the quality of a picture. (I have still less faith in such evidence today, when I catch sight of the tasteless colored caricatures of great works of art that disfigure the pages of our art magazines.) I entered the Refectory with a feeling approaching awe. The picture that I was about to see was one of those things that I had been taught to revere from my earliest childhood. It ranked in my mind with the church of St. Mark's in Venice and the Cathedral of Chartres, with Giotto's frescoes at Padua and Titian's great "Assumption," with the *Divina Commedia* and *Paradise Lost*. One did not criticize, I was told, such monuments of divinely inspired genius: one only wondered and worshiped. To carp at them was in bad taste: in fact it was almost akin to the sin of blasphemy.

Such an attitude in the presence of a popular masterpiece was by no means confined to the Victorian age. This kind of bigotry is rampant now, in a country and in a society in which the fashion of the passing moment counts for so much. To utter one word of honest criticism today in the presence of a picture that has been idolized by the hot gospelers of popular art coteries is clearly regarded, by many persons, as unseemly, if not actually indecent.

The feeling of disappointment that I experienced when I first caught sight of the "Last Supper" was somewhat mitigated when I contemplated the central figure of the composition; but it was by no means entirely removed. As far as one spectator was concerned, the artist had failed in his purpose. He had not conveyed to me the tremendous import of the event that he had portrayed, or his own inmost feelings in regard to it. In fact— to compare greater events with lesser—I suffered the same kind of disappointment that I experienced in later years when I looked at that extraordinarily inefficient piece of ideological propaganda, Picasso's "Guernica."

I would not have considered my own callow reactions in the presence of the "Last Supper" to be worth recording here, had they not received ample confirmation, in subsequent visits to Milan, and did I not know that other connoisseurs, possessed of a fine taste and an open mind, had suffered an experience similar to mine.

The "Last Supper" was begun by Leonardo in the year 1496 and was finished before February 8, 1498, when it was seen by Luca Pacioli, the great mathematician.[1] Leonardo did not choose for representation, as other artists had done, the supreme moment when Christ instituted the Holy Eucharist. He took his subject from the Gospel According to St. Luke. He portrayed the scene that followed Christ's utterance of the terrible words: "But look! the hand of him that betrays me is on the table." St. Luke tells us that, on hearing these words, the Apostles began to inquire among themselves who it was that should do this thing. And he is the only Evangelist who records that the hand of Judas as well as of Our Lord was on the table at the moment that the Apostle's treachery was revealed. Is it fanciful to suppose that Leonardo preferred to follow the account of the event given by St. Luke, rather than that of any other Evangelist, because St. Luke—if tradition does not lie—had the eye of an artist, and the trained mind of a physician, a student of natural science?

The "Last Supper" is a mural painting, but it was not ex-

[1] L. Beltrami, *Documenti e Memorie riguardanti la Vita e le Opere di Leonardo da Vinci* (Milan, 1919), p. 48. Pacioli speaks of the picture in his dedication to his book, *La Divina Proportione* (Venice, 1509).

ecuted in *buon fresco*. As in the case of the "Battle of Anghiari," painted some years later, Leonardo did not consider sufficiently the means to be employed in his work. He had not fully tested the medium that he proposed to use; nor had he examined the state of the wall on which the picture was to be painted. The wall of the new Refectory proved to be damp; and its surface was not properly prepared for painting. As a consequence, the "Last Supper" had already begun to perish but twenty years after it was finished.

When Vasari saw the picture, in the year 1556, it was already in a ruined state: It was, he tells us, a "muddle of blots." This testimony was fully confirmed by later witnesses. There is, in fact, abundant evidence to show that, in the seventeenth century, hardly a trace of Leonardo's original work remained. For, in addition to the testimony of those who then saw the picture, we have the more precise evidence of the early copies of the heads of the Apostles—drawings that were made from the original fresco by different pupils of the master—as well as the evidence of those copies of the complete work that were painted by Marco d'Oggiono. These contemporary reproductions clearly show how large a part of what we see today is the work of generations of restorers. Not only have the expressions of several of the faces been changed, but also, in some cases, the attitudes and gestures of the figures. The picture, in fact, has been drastically repainted many times.

Cavenaghi, the Milanese picture-restorer, when he was engaged upon the most recent of the many restorations of the "Last Supper," was wont to express the opinion that a considerable part of Leonardo's handiwork still remains. Although I had great respect for Cavenaghi, I was unable at the time to accept his conclusions, in view of the overwhelming evidence to the contrary, and also because I have found that the testimony of even the most competent restorers regarding the age of old paint is wholly unreliable. Cavenaghi believed what he said; and he knew his job better, perhaps, than did any of his contemporaries; but his testimony was, in reality, of little value. For, as I have proved many times in more recent years, a restorer is unable to distinguish between the work of the painter himself and that of some ingenious imitator. I can recall more than one occasion on which an official restorer of a great European gallery, a man of much knowledge and experience, was seriously deceived as to the age of a painting, pronouncing a modern fake to be more than four hundred years old. And these opinions were by no means hurriedly or carelessly given; for, in one case the picture was submitted to him by the trustees of his own gallery and ultimately purchased by them; and, in another case, he actually bought the picture, after due consideration, with his own money.

Nor are modern scientific tests infallible. The experts of a modern academy of art, using all the proper apparatus of modern scientific research, recently pronounced to be genuine a modern falsification, of which the origin and history are now known.

In face, then, of all the contradictory statements in regard to the present condition of the "Last Supper," there is one fact of which we can be certain: This picture, as we see it today, is not an original work; for very little, if any, of the master's own paint is now visible. Throughout four centuries, successive generations of restorers, some of them impiously self-opinionated, have interposed their personalities between the spectator and the master.

The "Last Supper," as a subject, presents great difficulties to the artist. Tintoretto alone, of all the great masters of the High Renaissance, succeeded in making an impressive picture out of a theme of this kind. Working at a rapid pace with few preliminary sketches, he succeeded in getting his vision onto canvas before it had faded, and before the emotions that created it had become cold.

Leonardo's method has been described in detail by Matteo Bandello, the *novelliere*—who knew the artist, and whose uncle was, as we have said, the Prior of the Convent of Santa Maria delle Grazie—in a well-known passage:

"Many times have I watched Leonardo go, in the early morning, and mount the platform that had been placed in the refectory, because the fresco that was being painted was at some height above the floor. There he was accustomed to remain from the rising of the sun until the dusk of evening, never laying down his brush, and refusing to eat or drink, he continued his painting. After that he might continue for three or four days without putting a hand to his work. Nevertheless, he would spend one or two hours of each of these days looking at the figures in his picture, meditating upon them, examining them, and then passing judgment upon them. I have also seen him, as the mood took him, leave the Corte Vecchia, when engaged on the clay model of his stupendous Horse, and go straight to the Convento delle Grazie, mount the platform there, take his brush in his hand, and give one or two touches to a figure. Then he would immediately quit the refectory, and take his departure from the Convent."[2]

Leonardo certainly gave more persistent, more continuous effort to the work on the "Last Supper" than he did to many of his pictures. But, in this period at Milan, as at other times, he had undertaken far more commissions, of different kinds, than he could possibly execute satisfactorily.

Leonardo succeeded, we have seen, in giving a certain unity to his work by choosing the most dramatic moment of that evening of tremendous events—happenings which have had a greater effect on the religious, and even the political, history of the world than those of any other evening in history, except the night when Christ was born. But Leonardo did not succeed in making the whole work convincing. It appears to me to resemble some carefully rehearsed scene in a great stage play, in which the characters had been posed by an experienced but unimaginative producer, working as he believed, in the classical tradition, but, in reality, influenced by a style that was far removed from that of the golden age of classical art. To us of a later day, these bulky, portentous figures, with their exaggerated gestures, recall the tumid bombast of certain sculptured representations of the potentates of Imperial Rome.

[2] M. Bandello, *Novelle* (Lucca, 1554), pp. 363, 364. This passage must refer to Leonardo's activities in the latter part of 1496 or the early months of 1497. See Appendix IV.

Professor Lionello Venturi has sought to defend the "Last Supper" from the charge of theatricality that has been leveled against it.[3] He argues that the gestures of the Apostles are deemed excessive and vulgar today because of the shortcomings of such contemporary copyists as Marco d'Oggiono, who have suppressed "le ombre dolcie e sfumose," "le ombre quasi insensibili," of Leonardo, that originally made less ostentatious, less monumental, the gesticulations of the twelve disciples and that unified the whole composition. In the copies and prints of the "Last Supper," as in Rubens' version of the "Battle of the Standard," another personality intervenes between us and the artist. Nor can we rely, he maintains, on the evidence afforded by the picture as we see it today. We must have recourse to other works of the artist himself, such as the "Adoration of the Magi" and the "Virgin of the Rocks," if we wish to reconstruct for ourselves that great dramatic painting, the "Last Supper."

In the eloquent plea of Venturi there is a modicum of truth, but there is also some exaggeration. For example, he is not entirely just to Marco d'Oggiono. Marco was certainly a third-rate artist; but he was a devoted and trusted follower of his great master; and, in making his three copies of the "Last Supper," he did his best to reproduce the picture faithfully. We ought, I think, to treat these copies with some respect.

I must confess, too, that I am a little disappointed because so conscientious a critic failed to warn the student that in the "Virgin of the Rocks," as we see it today, we cannot enjoy those "infinite gradations of light"[4] which Leonardo sought to paint, nor the delicate tones of its original colors.

Other writers have sought to excuse the exaggerated gesticulations of Leonardo's representations of the Apostles by assuring us that they are characteristically Italian and that they seem excessive only to cold Nordic critics. But this will not do. Other Italian artists, such as Tintoretto, have painted emo-

[3] L. Venturi, *La Critica e l'Arte di Leonardo da Vinci* ("Pubblicazioni dell'Istituto di Studi Vinciani in Roma" [Bologna, 1919]), pp. 191–95.

[4] J. P. and Irma A. Richter, *The Literary Works of Leonardo da Vinci* (London, 1939), I, 330.

tional scenes—scenes that hold us and enthral us. In all the paintings on the walls of San Rocco there is not one that strikes us as being theatrical or insincere. Nay more! Leonardo himself succeeded in making the passionate gestures and attitudes of the Wise Men and Prophets in the "Adoration of the Magi" entirely convincing. Let it be granted that the "Last Supper" is a difficult subject for any painter. Nevertheless, there must be some reason why, in this picture, so consummate an artist fails to convince us of the depth and the sincerity of the emotions that inspired it. What that reason was, it is not for me to say.

There is, however, one figure in Leonardo's "Last Supper" that is still entirely convincing. Calm amidst the storm of excited feeling, recollected, sympathetic, yet full of innate majesty, the central figure dominates the whole scene. Here, at last, the artist succeeded. This figure alone, notwithstanding its present condition, shows us that Leonardo did not altogether fail in his great task.

CHAPTER XI

LEONARDO'S PICTURES
THE LAST FLORENTINE PERIOD

THE cartoon of the "Madonna and St. Anne" which is in London was, we believe, the first work that Leonardo made when he returned to Florence, after nearly twenty years' absence, in the spring of the year 1500.[1] This drawing is generally regarded as the most beautiful of all his works. In it the artist gives perfect expression to those human emotions which, from his earliest years, had moved him most deeply— the love of a mother for her child. Here, at least, he makes an entirely artistic use of all that he had learned about chiaroscuro and contraposto. The whole cartoon is as spontaneous, as sincere, as his early drawings of the Madonna and Child. But since that early time he has added greatly to his means of expression. This cartoon is in his Cinquecento style. Not only has the artist acquired a greater facility in rendering light and shade, and movement: in the drapery of his figures we find a plastic quality that has rarely been equaled.

The altarpiece commissioned by the Servites was not painted. The first cartoon that Leonardo made had not, it seems, satisfied his ecclesiastical patrons. The second cartoon had received general approval; but, after making it, the artist had become immersed in other occupations. "He is absorbed in the study of geometry," writes Fra Pietro da Novellara, "and hates the sight of a brush." But, several years later, Leonardo characteristically returned again to the subject, and designed, and in part painted, the "Madonna and St. Anne" which is now in the Louvre, a work which lacks the simplicity, tenderness, and spontaneity of the vision that the master recorded when, after many years of absence, he returned to his own country, to that smiling Tuscan land in which he had passed his childhood.

Like all such cartoons, that which is at Burlington House

[1] See n. 4, chap. iii; also Appendix V.

has suffered serious injury. But enough of the original work remains to give us unalloyed pleasure. For once the Florentine artist's devotion to science was not allowed to interfere with the exercise of his primary vocation.

Another great work that Leonardo began soon after his return to Florence was the portrait of "Monna Lisa," the third wife of a well-known citizen of Florence. "Leonardo undertook to paint for Francesco del Giocondo," writes Vasari, "a portrait of Monna Lisa his wife; and, after he had lingered over it for four years, he left it unfinished. By looking at this picture, whoever wishes to see how closely art can imitate nature can learn at once what can be done; for, in it, we see counterfeited all the minutest details that it is possible to paint. . . . . The eyes have the lustre and liquid sheen that are seen in real life; and around them are those rosy and pearly tints . . . . that cannot be reproduced except with the utmost subtlety. . . . . The nose with its beautiful nostrils, rosy and tender, seems to be alive. The mouth . . . . united by the red of the lips to the flesh tones of the face, appears not to be painted but living flesh." As we read Vasari's words, we realize that, since Leonardo's day, the aspect of the picture has entirely changed, and that, like some other works of the master, it has been covered with successive layers of dirt and old varnish that have concealed its beautiful colors and have hidden its subtle, almost imperceptible gradations of tone.

I am firmly convinced that Vasari's account of the "Monna Lisa" is based on personal knowledge.[2] But even if it were proved that he had not seen the picture itself, and that he knew it only through the medium of copies and the descriptions of other artists, we must still treat his account of it with respect, in view of the fact that he knew well Francesco Melzi, a man of fine taste and himself an artist, whose life's mission it was to preserve faithfully his master's works and to hand them on to posterity.

If we wish to have a clear knowledge of Leonardo's style, it is of the highest importance that we should allow Vasari's account of the "Monna Lisa" to sink into our minds. Otherwise,

[2] See Appendix VI.

we may be deluded into accepting an entirely mistaken view of Leonardo's *sfumato* manner. When I stand opposite the veiled portrait of Francesco del Giocondo's young wife, I recall the words: "The eyes had that lustre and liquid sheen that we see in real life; and around them are those rosy and pearly tints . . . . that cannot be reproduced except with the utmost subtlety." Leonardo, we repeat, gave to the word *sfumato* a connotation entirely different from that which some writers on art have given to it. It is true that, as Corot, in a later day, loved to paint in the cool hours that follow the dawn, so Leonardo, "wishing to give the highest relief to the things which he executed," sometimes chose to paint in the evening twilight. But the pictures that he then created had none of the muddy tones that disfigure today all of his most important paintings, and that lead the unwary to give an entirely exaggerated meaning to the word *sfumato*.

The portrait of La Gioconda has indeed been shamefully treated, not only in distant ages, but also in the present century. Like "pious Aeneas," it has been "much tossed about." Torn away from the walls of the Louvre by a thief, on August 21, 1911, it was then taken to Florence. Recovered, after more than two years of absence, it was not permitted to remain long in its old home. For, in the autumn of 1914, it was interred in some secure place, and remained there until the end of the first World War. When I was shown the picture after its return to the Louvre, it seemed to me to be darker and dirtier than ever.

It is a continual source of wonder to me that art historians as a class pay so little attention to the condition of paintings. Some of the most eminent of them have bestowed the highest praise on pictures by great artists that have been entirely repainted, and that in their present state of preservation are little better than copies. The condition of the "Monna Lisa," thank God! is far better than that. Its original beauties are by no means entirely hidden from view. But we see them "as through a glass darkly." And this fact—though they would not admit it even to themselves—has influenced the opinions that some modern critics have formed of it. But that the "Monna Lisa" deserved, in some measure, the encomiums of Vasari is clear from the fact that it was so highly esteemed by other artists, and by the art-loving people of Florence. No picture of that great age of art received a more enthusiastic reception. No picture of the time has been more frequently copied.

Married in the year 1495, at the age of sixteen, Monna Lisa soon lost her only child. Her portrait was painted during the time that Leonardo was in Florence after his return from Milan, that is to say between April 24, 1500, and May 30, 1506, and was begun, Milanesi concludes, very soon after her bereavement.

Vasari, in a passage already quoted, states that Leonardo worked for four years on the picture. There is evidence that points to the conclusion that the artist, in the course of these years, made important modifications in his original design. The subject of his portrait changed, and the artist's vision of her also changed.

We can trace two distinct stages in the creation of the portrait. At first, when he made a cartoon for this picture, Leonardo's intention was to paint Francesco del Giocondo's sad young wife as a saint, holding in her hand a lily.[3] Later on, having discarded this idea, he decided to represent her as a worldly young matron, looking out on the world from the loggia of her palace, and having as a background an Alpine valley, flanked on either side by lofty peaks.

It is probable, as we have said, that the portrait of Monna Lisa was commissioned in the year 1500, or early in 1501, when its subject was about twenty-one years of age, and that the cartoon was made about the same time. In this drawing, the lady appears as somewhat more slender and less developed, as well as more melancholy, than in the finished picture. There is, too, a slight difference in her pose.

The work on the picture was interrupted for at least nine months, when Leonardo left Florence in May, 1502, to serve as a military engineer under Caesar Borgia. When the artist had drawn his cartoon, the young mother was still mourning over

[3] For the history of this cartoon see above, p. 39.

the loss of her child. After his return to Florence from Romagna, he found her somewhat changed. Her figure was more buxom; she was more self-assured, a woman of the world, disillusioned and somewhat cynical. It was at that time that Leonardo discarded the idea of representing her as a saint. He resolved to portray La Gioconda as he then saw her, with a revealing smile on her handsome face. The background that he paints is clearly reminiscent of the Upper Engadine Valley, as seen from the higher slopes of Muottas Murail.

The picture was left unfinished. For in the latter part of this sojourn in Florence, in the years 1504 and 1505, Leonardo was much occupied with other projects, and more especially with works that he had undertaken for his native city, such as the great fresco of the "Battle of Anghiari." This mural decoration he had been commissioned to paint, by the Signoria, in the Sala di Gran Consiglio of the Palazzo Vecchio.

Much has been written about Monna Lisa's enigmatic smile. But there is, in reality, nothing mysterious about it; for, in the first place, the smile was one of the stock properties of the studio of Verrocchio, a property that was taken over by his chief pupil, when the master left Florence. Just as in the studio of the Victorian photographer it was a general rule that, when anyone sat for a portrait, he should smile, so it was in the studio in which Leonardo received his artistic training.

But it would be entirely unjust to Leonardo to say that his chief aim in endeavoring to make the lady smile was identical with that of the commercial photographer of the last century. He had a deeper purpose: His object was to "reveal the passions of the soul." He wished "to catch Monna Lisa off her guard." —He knew well that a smile, like good wine, may be a revealer. Like wine, it can bring into a stronger light the kindliness of the good, the vulgarity of the vulgar, the quiet despair of the disillusioned, and the concealed malevolence of the bad.

Leonardo had some difficulty in attaining his object. At first, when he made the cartoon, the smile of the young mother was almost imperceptible. She was obviously unhappy. Later on, when he got down to the job of painting his picture, he felt that something must be done about it. The lady, still melancholy, though more self-possessed than heretofore, must be made to smile. Therefore, just as the Victorian photographer was wont to produce a squeaking teddy-bear, or a monkey-on-a-stick, when an infant remained obstinately glum, so Leonardo engaged musicians and buffoons to make the lady smile. At last he attained his object. Monna Lisa's smile tells us quite a lot about her.

The portrait of Monna Lisa has been the subject of paeans of praise from Vasari's time to the age of Walter Pater. Some of these entirely sincere encomiums have naturally come from critics who were infected with Florentine *campanilismo*, that is to say, from writers who had been accustomed to accept without question the estimates of works of the Florentine school that had been made by patriotic Florentines and their disciples.

In more recent years, on the other hand, the "Monna Lisa" has been the subject of somewhat frivolous criticism. One distinguished critic confesses that he does "not like the woman." He admits, with charming candor, that he thinks her watchful, sly, secure, self-satisfied, and, above all, supercilious. "She was," he says, "unlike the women that he had known and dreamt of": he would not wish to add her to his circle of feminine friends. In his case, her unfortunate character effectually prevented that "mystic union . . . . which is the essence of the aesthetic moment." He was relieved, he tells us, when he heard that the "Monna Lisa" had been stolen, and that he would not see her face again.[4]

If such methods of criticism were generally adopted and carried to their logical conclusion, where would they land us? Would some critics suborn gangsters to purloin and destroy such pictures as annoyed them? I, myself, do not like the woman painted by El Greco in his representations of "St. Mary Magdalen"; and I detest the "Battista Sforza" of Piero della Francesca's portrait. These are not at all the kind of women that I would like to number amongst my intimate friends. Should I, then, rejoice if either of these pictures were stolen

---

[4] B. Berenson, *Study and Criticism of Italian Art* [*Third Series*] (London, 1916).

from the public gallery which is now its home? Would I, for example, take pleasure in the thought that I was never to see it again? Far from it! I was genuinely sorry when the "St. Mary Magdalen," now at Worcester, left London for another hemisphere. Notwithstanding Monna Lisa's unsympathetic character, I love to contemplate her portrait. For, in painting this portrait, a great artist did not become exhausted before his long and painful method of creating a picture had accomplished something approaching a perfect expression of his feelings about its subject. With marvelous technical skill he has put before us his vision of a woman of the High Renaissance. Self-satisfied, worldly, watchful, feline, a little disdainful—all these epithets she undoubtedly deserves. But, highly civilized though she appears to be, she remains *au fond* a primitive human female. "The last animal to be civilized by man will be woman." This background, then, of untamed nature, of rugged mountains and well-watered valleys, is not without its symbolical significance. I find in it something akin to the pathetic fallacy.

We are not in love with Monna Lisa, as, I think, Leonardo was not in love with her. But she interests us immensely; and we realize, or think that we realize, what it was that the great master felt about her. In a creative career in which there were some abortions, and some imperfect offspring, the artist has given birth to a well-nigh perfect child.

Of the "Battle of Anghiari," it is not possible to give any adequate description. Nor am I able in discussing the picture to fulfil the function of a critic. I cannot say whether the artist realized his own artistic purpose in painting it; nor can I attempt to define its peculiar virtue, or explain why it gives me a certain quality of pleasure. For, as a picture, the "Battle of Anghiari" has never existed. Only a small part of it was finished; and that part I know only on the evidence of a rather pedestrian copy, and of a copy of a copy that was made by Rubens—in which case a highly individual personality intervenes between me and Leonardo.

But I can clearly understand why it was that Leonardo chose

this subject. Being something of a pacifist, he wished, as I have said, to portray "the bestial frenzy of war." There were other reasons, too, why he was interested in a cavalry battle and wished to give to the world a representation of it. He was the son of an ambitious and successful burgher. Like other men with a similar social background, he showed, from an early age, a keen interest in horses. In Europe, from the time of the Romans until yesterday, the horse was a kind of social symbol. In English cavalry regiments, a considerable proportion of the officers were the sons of successful lawyers, brewers, and moneylenders, who were ambitious that their offspring should occupy a place in the class of *equites*.

From the beginning of his career as an independent artist, until his last days in Milan, he was frequently making drawings of horses. In other ways he was anxious to show that he was not—to borrow a phrase of a bishop much loved by the Cavaliers—"a low mechanic fellow." He explains very carefully, in the *Trattato*, that painting was a very gentlemanly occupation as compared with sculpture. "The painter," he says, "sits down to work entirely at his ease, and well-dressed, and handles a light brush dipped in refined colours. He arrays himself in whatever clothes he pleases. His house is clean and filled with pictures, and often he works to the accompaniment of music, or to the reading of beautiful literature." In this, as in many other things, Leonardo was not consistent. He expressed a profound contempt for wealth; but he demanded an environment that cannot be secure without the possession of a considerable share of it.

All the same, whilst we recognize the very human weaknesses of the artist, so naïvely expressed, we feel a genuine pang of regret that the most important commission that he ever received was never successfully executed. It is unfortunate, too, that we do not possess any representations of horses that are undoubtedly by him—either in painting or in sculpture—except those that are in the background of the "Adoration of the Magi." The numerous sketches of horses from his hand that have come down to us tend only to deepen our regret.

CHAPTER XII

LEONARDO'S LAST PICTURES

OF ALL the pictures that Leonardo painted in the last thirteen years of his life, only two have survived: the "Virgin and Child and St. Anne" and the "St. John the Baptist," both of which are in the Louvre. His career as a painter did not end gloriously. It is not true of him, as it is of Fra Angelico and Giovanni Bellini, of Titian and Rembrandt, that the works that the artist painted in his old age are amongst his finest creations. In fact, the "St. John the Baptist" is, perhaps, his least satisfactory picture.

But, whilst the "Madonna and St. Anne" and the "St. John the Baptist" are not amongst Leonardo's masterpieces, each of them, in its own way, supports his claim to be an innovator, a pioneer. For the "Virgin and Child and St. Anne" is a complicated exercise in *contraposto;* and the "St. John the Baptist," darker than most of his pictures really are, is the most pronounced, if not the most subtle, example of the *sfumato* manner.

Without doubt, Leonardo made the cartoon for the "Virgin and Child and St. Anne," his third cartoon of this subject; but the execution of the picture at the Louvre is, in great part, the work of a pupil. As a consequence, whilst the brush-work of the painting is tame and undistinguished, its design is an impressive manifestation of virtuosity. This design, in fact, gives me the same quality of pleasure as does the solo performance of some brilliant violinist of the concert halls, who earns prolonged applause by a display of amazing dexterity.

Psychologically, too, the picture at the Louvre is disappointing. Instead of feeling exalted, as we should do, at the contemplation of a work with such a subject by a great master, we are distracted by the unnatural, uncomfortable postures of the two adult figures in the composition. As we look at the picture, we see that it represents a heavy, large-limbed woman, seated firmly on the lap of her parent. The artist, it is true, has sought to reassure us by putting a smile on the face of the older woman. We feel, nevertheless, that Leonardo, in his masterly treatment of *contraposto* has become a little inhuman, if not irreverent.

Owing to a happier disposition of the figures, the cartoon in London does not give us the same unpleasant impression. In the earlier work we find a blither, lighter young woman, with one foot firmly planted on the ground. More than that, the force and spontaneity of the whole drawing, its abundant charm, and its amazing technical qualities, lead us to forget all minor blemishes.

The "St. John the Baptist" is not only an exercise in chiaroscuro, it is an epitome of all the old master's pet morphological details—the pointing finger, the loose, abundant hair, the smile, that ever recurring smile, that here, even more than in his other works, reveals only too clearly "the passions of the soul" of the real subject of the picture. Like some popular favorite of the variety stage, some old trouper giving his valedictory performance, Leonardo repeats all his accustomed tricks to the great delight of his loyal admirers.

But the "St. John the Baptist" is something more than an exercise in chiaroscuro and an epitome of the artist's morphological mannerisms; it is an expression of some of Leonardo's deeper feelings. "Art," Yeats confided to me one day in Merrion Square, "is the child of desire—*the desire of one's opposite.*" This aphorism is not universally true, Rembrandt's self-portraits of his last period are certainly amongst his best works. Some of them, such as the Kinnaird portrait, are far superior as works of art to the portraits of the little serving-maid he loved. Fra Angelico, himself a holy man, painted saints far more successfully than he painted sinners. But it is undoubtedly true of Leonardo. A superman, if ever there was one, a man, too, of great physical strength and beauty, he loved to paint decadent, androgynous types.

He acted most certainly within his rights as an artist in portraying such subjects. But when he gave to a portrait of a person of this type the title "St. John the Baptist," he not only made a mistake, he was guilty of a crime. For his picture represents no holy personage, but some creature of dubious sex, some minister of vice, with bare arms and shoulders, peering out of the encircling darkness, and pointing upward with his right hand. But for the slender cross that he carries, who would imagine that this figure was intended to be a representation of a saint? And who would imagine that the holy person represented was the heroic young pioneer of a new religion, who rebuked the vices of a tyrant, and who went on foot from one end of his native land to the other, exhorting his fellow-countrymen to repentance?

The apologetics of recent critics who have written on the "St. John the Baptist" remind me forcibly—in more than one respect—of many sermons that I heard in the last century from Victorian pulpits, from the lips of unwary advocates, who had not grasped the simple fact that men will believe the impossible but not the improbable. Such discourses only confirmed the doubts of some of their listeners.

To say of this picture that in making it the artist has vamped up an old design of an Announcing Angel does not help in any way to mitigate the charge that has been brought against Leonardo. For, if it is grossly unjust to give to a picture of some obviously vicious person the title, "St. John the Baptist," it would be far more unseemly—all things considered—to portray such a creature as the Angel Gabriel, the Angel of the Annunciation. For the Angel Gabriel has attained celestial perfection, whilst the young prophet who called his fellow-countrymen to repentance was still—as St. Paul confessed himself to be—an erring, mortal man. Change a little the gestures of this figure: call it the Angel Gabriel, if you will; it still remains an outrage against decency. For such a lampoon is not only calculated to wound the feelings of sincere Christians: it is an offense against the fundamental doctrines of humanism. And the most tragic thing about the whole history of this picture is that, as far as we know, it roused no protests from the Christian world on its first appearance. In fact, when it was shown to a

Cardinal of the Church, at the Castle of Cloux, he regarded it as "most perfect." That, at least, is the epithet bestowed on the "St. John the Baptist" by his faithful secretary and companion, Antonio de' Beatis.

Many years ago, I ventured to express the opinion that Leonardo, whilst he was one of the greatest of men, was not one of the greatest of painters. A venerable Italian critic who was present raised his hands in horror, exclaiming: "Bestemmia! Bestemmia!" Many of the opinions that I held in those long-distant days were mistaken; but I do not think that I was in error about Leonardo. He did not so completely express himself as an artist as did, for example, Michelangelo and Rembrandt, Titian and Tintoretto. He was, it is true, one of the world's greatest draughtsmen. It must be confessed, however, that some small part of his acknowledged supremacy is due to the fact that so many of his drawings have survived. The pious Melzi rendered Leonardo and posterity an inestimable service.

Notwithstanding the fact that Leonardo produced but few pictures of the highest class, he exercised a considerable influence over his contemporaries, as well as over the artists of the next generation. Raphael and Giorgione, Dürer and Correggio—all owed something to Leonardo. For, in some respects, he was an innovator, a pioneer, who helped to blaze the trail that other leaders of art movements were destined to follow. He was a pioneer in the treatment of light and shade. He was amongst the pioneers in the art of landscape. He was a pioneer, too, in that he sought to get movement into his works, by rhythmic, contrasted curves that lead the eye of the spectator into the background of the picture. Harmonious movement and depth—these are the things that he strove to create.

Whilst we cannot agree that Leonardo, as an artist, merits the unquestioning awe that was once accorded to him, it must be admitted that, as a man, he fills us with wonder, as he did the men of his own time. On no other mortal have ever been bestowed so many rare gifts. For this reason, men will never cease to take an interest in his life and his works.

APPENDIX I

"THE MADONNA DI PIAZZA"

Archivio Com. di Pistoia, Libri di Provisioni, Cod. 68:—"Fu per li executori del testamento della felice memoria di Mons. Nostro Donato de Medici vostro degnissimo Vescovo, prestantissimi consiglieri, allogato a fare una tavola da altare a Andrea del Verrochio da Firenze per l'altare dell' oratorio della Vergine di piaza: la quale si dice esser facta o mancarvi pocho et è più di sei anni l'harebbe finita se da detti executori havesse avuto interamente el debito suo: che ne resta havere l. 253 che havuto per insino alla somma di fl. 60 larghi. Dicesi essere una bellissima cosa e condocta a quel termine che v'è con grandi arti: et venendo non sarebbe se non a honore et ornamento della vostra città e accrescimento di devotione di quel luogo. Et come sanno ogni giorno le prestantie vostre fanno elemosina ad altri: sieno contenti questa volta farla a se medesimo perocchè detto oratorio è dell'op. vostra di Sant' Iacopo et immediate sottoposto al ghoverno di quella e non d'altri proverete che detta tavola vengha. Il perchè sia riformata e vinto che e' presenti operai habbino auctorità di vedere se dicta tavola è secondo la scripta e disegno in quella dato e non essendo finita farla finire et bisognando pagare a dicto Andrea al presente di quello si sta havere per insino alla somma di fl. sei larghi gli paghino della massa di detta opera mettendo acconto di dicto Andrea: et ogni suo resto promettino et obblighino l'opera a pagarli per tutto el mese d'ottobre proximo advenire. Et sieno tenuti a farla venire, et pervenuta che sarà, a farla porre al luogo pio, pagando l'opera vectura et gabelle secondo eran tenuti detti executori: et quanto perciò pagasseno, come è detto, sia admesso da loro ragioni.

Die 21 Novembre firmata fn. 10.[1]

Die 22 Novembre comprobata fn. 17.

Die 25 Novembre in consilio obtenta fn. 69 fb. 9."

---

[1] November, 1485. This document was first published by Alfredo Chiti, in the *Bollettino Storico Pistoiese*, I (1899), 2. See also M. Cruttwell, *Verrocchio* (London, 1904), pp. 254, 255.

APPENDIX II
"THE MADONNA OF THE CAT"

A brief note by Leonardo which is in the *Codice Atlantico* tells us that he was once in prison.[1] Here is the complete note: "When I made a Christ Child you put me in prison: now if I represent him grown up, you will treat me worse." J. P. Richter came to the conclusion that this sentence refers to a lost picture, the "Madonna del Gatto": he held the opinion that the Inquisition regarded this picture as irreverent if not blasphemous. With this view I cannot agree. In some other pictures of the "Madonna and Child," as well as in certain works that represent scenes from the life of the Virgin— and also in some popular miracle plays—we find just as realistic a treatment of religious subjects as we do in the drawings for the "Madonna of the Cat."[2] Moreover, in this note Leonardo does not state that the subject of the offending work of art was a "Madonna and Child." He speaks of it as a "Christ Child"; and, from the wording of the passage, it seems possible that it may have been a piece of sculpture.

But there is another reason why it is difficult to accept the hypothesis that the sentence that I have quoted above refers to the lost "Madonna of the Cat." We know that it was characteristic of Leonardo as an artist to take up an old theme of his, and to make something that was no mere reproduction of an earlier work but an entirely new creation—something that expressed what the artist felt about the original theme at the time that he began to make the new picture. Now there are at the British Museum not only some of his early drawings for a "Madonna of the Cat"—sketches which date from about 1478[3]—there are also in that collection two other drawings of the same subject that clearly belong to a later date in a period of rapid development.[4] These later drawings are not the sketches from life of an artist who is collecting material for a picture but finished studies: in each of them, Leonardo has drawn the outline of a frame. The two studies were made in the year 1482, or perhaps a little later. If Leonardo had been imprisoned for painting a "Madonna of the Cat" in 1478, is it likely that, but a few years later, he would set to work on a second picture with the same subject?

[1] *Codice Atlantico*, 252a; J. P. and Irma A. Richter, *The Literary Works of Leonardo da Vinci* (Oxford University Press, 1939), II, 342, No. 1364.

[2] E. Bodmer, *Disegni di Leonardo* (Florence, 1939), Pls. 2 and 3; also H. Bodmer, *Leonardo da Vinci: Des Meisters Gemälde und Zeichnungen* ("Klassiker der Kunst" Series [Stuttgart, 1931]), pp. 121–24.

[3] See Pl. XXV.

[4] These later drawings have been frequently reproduced in books on Leonardo (see H. Bodmer, *Leonardo*, pp. 161, 162, and 280).

APPENDIX III
THE "VIRGIN OF THE ROCKS" IN THE NATIONAL GALLERY

There are good reasons for believing that Leonardo, in his two Milanese periods, accepted commissions for pictures that were painted wholly, or in great part in his studio, by his assistants. The "Virgin of the Rocks" in the National Gallery is one of these pictures.

This work, which was not originally designed as a triptych, but as an altarpiece of five panels, is obviously the work of two hands. The side panels are, by general admission, the work of a pupil. The center panel, though it approaches in some respects more nearly to Leonardo's later *sfumato* style, was actually painted by one of his assistants. This becomes clear if we set this panel by the side of the picture with the same subject that is in the Louvre. We are at once struck by the extraordinary difference in the quality of the two paintings. The artist who painted the picture in London has attempted, of course, to imitate his master's later *sfumato* style, but in how heavy-handed a fashion! We find in his work none of that infinite subtlety in the gradation of tones, none of that ultra-sensitive, plastic quality that we see in those works that are by Leonardo's own hand.

It is true that in the head of the Angel we can discover a lighter, more sensitive touch. Here, when painting in his master's studio—with perhaps a cartoon of Leonardo before him—the artist who painted it succeeded in producing finer gradations of light and shade than in the rest of the picture; and this has led some recent writers on Leonardo to conclude that the master himself had a hand in the painting of the altarpiece.[1]

It is, of course, possible that Leonardo gave some finishing touches to the center panel; though, taken as a whole, the work itself seems to contradict that hypothesis. Even the head of the Angel in the "Virgin of the Rocks" does not fully confirm it. And, we may add, the shadowgraph of this detail, when closely studied, raises more doubts regarding its authorship than it dispels; for it reveals weakness in those very elements in which Leonardo's own work is peculiarly strong. The long nose of the Angel is not faultlessly attached to the cheek. The lower lip and chin are not modeled with the same assurance that they are in the head of the Virgin in the Burlington House cartoon. In a word the handling here is somewhat fumbling. The artist, in fact, has given the Angel something resembling an incipient double chin. The whole

---

[1] A. Burroughs, *Art Criticism from a Laboratory* (Boston, 1938), pp. 82–88. Kenneth Clark, *Leonardo da Vinci* (Cambridge University Press, 1939), p. 142.

representation does not possess the force, the plastic unity, of the figure of the Madonna in that supreme work of art, the Cartoon at the Royal Academy. We feel as we look at it that a painstaking pupil has made here a brave attempt to emulate the excellencies of his master's style; but it is an effort that leaves us quite cold.

One recent writer on Leonardo contends that the "Virgin of the Rocks" in London must be by the master himself because we find in it several *pentimenti*. But is it not far more probable, taking into account the general lack of quality in this work, and in view of the practices that prevailed at that time in the studio, that these corrections were suggested by Leonardo himself, when inspecting the work of a pupil?

Finally, there are good reasons for believing that Leonardo was much occupied with other work for the French king, during his second period of residence in Milan. It seems, indeed, that the reason that Louis gave for insisting on Leonardo's return to Milan was little more than a pretext. Stimulated by the new demands that were made upon him, Leonardo accepted more commissions than he could hope to execute. Once again, he displayed his chronic variability.

APPENDIX IV
MATTEO BANDELLO

To a student of the history of art, no less than to other historical students, the firsthand evidence of an intelligent, well-informed witness of great events is of primary importance. Matteo Bandello, the *novelliere*, a Dominican friar who was keenly interested in the arts, is such a witness. Both by temperament, and because of the opportunities that he enjoyed throughout a long life, he was peculiarly fitted for his chief function, that of a chronicler. Art historians are especially indebted to him because he gave us an eyewitness' account of Leonardo's methods in painting. In his youth[1] he knew the master, and had watched him when he was at work on the "Last Supper," in the convent of which Bandello's uncle was at that time the Prior. The future writer also knew Leonardo's chief patrons, Lodovico il Moro and Beatrice d'Este. For they were frequent visitors at Santa Maria delle Grazie, and were regular worshipers at the convent church.

Moreover, Bandello was well acquainted with other discriminating patrons of the arts. He was, for example, an intimate friend of the Duchess of Milan's famous sister, the most intelligent, the most ardent of all contemporary collectors and connoisseurs, Isabella d'Este; of whom it might be said that "to know her was a liberal education." For three years, he sat daily at her hospitable table, meeting there the artists and craftsmen that were then employed at the Court of Mantua. There, he conversed frequently with men of rare taste such as Baldassare Castiglione, the friend of Raphael.

Matteo Bandello is often described as a novelist. But the friar was not a novelist in the sense in which that word is generally understood today in Great Britain and America. He was not, that is to say, a writer of fiction. He would be more correctly described as a chronicler. It is true that he sometimes related old stories of events long past—"tales of loving ladies hapless haps, their deaths and deadly cares." It is true, also, that he sometimes repeated traditional accounts of events nearer to his own day, like the story of Fra Filippo Lippi's capture by Moorish pirates. But he always believed that the tales that he told were veracious histories. His primary function was to

[1] The date of Bandello's birth is not known. The Bull of his Nomination to the Bishopric of Agen, which is dated 1550, states that he is about sixty-five. But this is clearly a guess; as is a statement that he is sixty-five years old in a legal document of 1551. His suffragan, Giovanni Valerio, declared, in the same year, that Bandello was about eighty! One of his best biographers, D. Morellini, says that he was born in 1480. See D. Morellini, *Matteo Bandello, Novellatore Lombardo* (Sondrio, 1900); also A. Durangues, "Matteo Bandello," *Revue de l'Agenais*, July–August, 1933, pp. 196, 197.

record actual happenings. "The greater part of his *novelle*," writes Parodi, "derive their interest from the fact that the stories they narrate are materially true."

Moreover, it is not only in his *novelle* that we find much relevant information about the political and social history, the literature, and the art of his time. The dedicatory letters with which he prefaces each of his stories —letters addressed to friends belonging to all classes of the community—are sources of contemporary history of considerable importance.

Nor was it merely because he told true stories about other Italians of the High Renaissance that some of his works were translated by François de Belleforest and Geoffrey Fenton,[2] and were, as Roger Ascham testifies, eagerly read in England. His works had the added attraction that they were, in some cases, chronicles of events in which he had actually taken part. He himself, for example, had played a leading rôle in the tragical drama of the Countess of Celant, Marston's "Insatiate Countess."

I can, I think, claim to speak of Bandello with some authority, as I have spent a not inconsiderable amount of time, in the last fifty years, in researches in regard to his life and his writings. I realized from the first that, of all of the *novellieri*, none was more important to the historian than Bandello, for reasons that I have already indicated. Having this conviction, I endeavored to learn more about him and his circle in places where he had lived, such as Milan and Agen. Knowing something of Bandello and his works, it is surprising to me that the evidence of such a witness should be undervalued today by any serious student of art history.

[2] Sir Geoffrey Fenton, *Certaine Tragicall Discourses*, with an Introduction by R. Langton Douglas ("Tudor Translations Series" [London, 1898]).

APPENDIX V

SEBASTIANO RESTA

In a letter[1] written to Giampietro Bellori, Sebastiano Resta states that "Louis XII, King of France, before 1500, commissioned a cartoon of St. Anne from Leonardo da Vinci, 1695. In the same letter, he states that the artist made a second sketch in 1500, whilst he was still resident in Milan! There does not exist a vestige of contemporary evidence to support either of these statements. Nor can we find anything to substantiate the hypothesis that in making them Resta was quoting "an old tradition." They are, in fact, the unsupported assertions of a chronically inaccurate biographer, who, as we shall see, was accustomed to state as proved facts the most absurd and baseless theories regarding events that had occurred two hundred years before he had put pen to paper.

It is a surprising fact that this Lombard critic, who wrote a *Life* of Leonardo, and who posed as an authority on Milanese art, was amazingly ignorant regarding Leonardo's relations with Louis XII in the years 1506 to 1513, when the French ruled in Milan, and thus was wholly unaware of some of the most important events in the whole history of art in that Lombard city. He did not know, for example, that Leonardo was summoned to Milan by the French King in the summer of 1506, and that, except for one period of nine months, he remained there, working at first for Louis, and afterwards for his representatives, Charles d'Amboise and Gian Giacomo Trivulzio, throughout a period of seven years' duration.

We know that Resta thought that it was one of his missions in life to revise Vasari's biographical account of Leonardo da Vinci.[2] As a matter of fact, in every case where he attempted to correct some statement of the Aretine biographer, he blundered hopelessly. Knowing well on what flimsy foundations he based his confident statements regarding the facts of Leonardo's life, it is not difficult to arrive at a conclusion as to the origin of his allegation regarding the Burlington House cartoon. Resta knew that the cartoon was, at the time that he was writing, in the old collection of a great Milanese family, the Arconati. He therefore assumed that it had been made in Milan. Being vaguely aware that, at one time, Louis XII had employed Leonardo, he jumped to the conclusion that it was the French King who had commissioned Leonardo to make the St. Anne cartoon. He does not explain, how-

---

[1] M. Gio. Bottari, *Raccolta di Lettere sulla Pittura*, etc., III, 481. This letter was probably written in the year 1696, at the time that Resta was at work on his *Life of Leonardo da Vinci*.

[2] M. Gio. Bottari, *op. cit.*, III, 515–18.

ever, why it was that Louis XII, who was, at a later time, an enthusiastic admirer of the artist and a collector of his works, did not take possession of the masterpiece that, according to Resta's conjecture, the King had himself commissioned.

Resta's conclusion regarding the early history of the cartoon now in London was based, it seems, upon two unsound premises. For in the first place, the cartoon did not enter the Arconati collection until the year 1628. Before that, it had been in the great collection of drawings and cartoons that Melzi had inherited from Leonardo; and there are grounds for supposing that the master in his lifetime had kept this cartoon in his own private possession. Secondly, whilst Leonardo painted a small picture for one of Louis' courtiers as early as 1501, there is no reason to suppose that he received any commission from the King himself before the year 1506.

We do not exaggerate when we repeat that Sebastiano Resta is an utterly unreliable witness, and that any statement that he makes regarding Leonardo is of no value unless it can be demonstrated to be correct by the testimony of trustworthy witnesses. In order to prove this, we will reprint here, in full, Resta's *Succinct Account of the Life of Leonardo*, a summary of his biography of the artist. I venture to state that in all the innumerable biographical writings relating to the life of Leonardo there is no more ridiculous document:

"SUCCINTO RACCONTO DELLA VITA DI LIONARDO

Lionardo nasce circa l'anno 1467.

Sua puerizia di 14 anni, per far tutte quelle cose e quegli studi che racconta il Vasari.

In quest'anno, 1481, si messe alla scuola del Verrocchio sino al 1485.

Due anni sino al 1487, stette da per sè. In questo biennio suppongo che scappasse a Roma, e facesse la sua Madonna in s. Onofrio.

Va a Milano, e vi sta 13 anni, fino al 1500.

In quest'anno, fatto prigione il Moro, se ne torna a Firenze, e vi sta fino al 1513.

Va a Roma alla coronazione di Leon X.

Torna a Firenze nel 1515, e vi sta due anni sino al 1517.

Va in quest'anno in Francia, e vi dimora certamente fino al 1542, in cui Michelagnolo scoperse il suo Giudizio.

Ecco i punti che mi pare d'aver fissato con molte ragioni, e colle autorità di vari storici, da' quali punti ho ricevuto la correzione di molti sbagli, che me pare che abbiano preso coloro che hanno ragionato di Lionardo, e il modo di riordinare la Vita che ne scrive il Vasari confusamente."

We see then that the researches that Resta engaged in, to establish the main facts of Leonardo's life, and to correct the errors of Vasari, led him to the following conclusions: He tells us that the artist was born in the year

1467 and that it was not until 1481 that Leonardo (who, we know, was admitted to full membership in the Guild of Painters in 1472) began his apprenticeship in Verrocchio's school. He asserts that it was in the year 1487 that Leonardo went to Milan, and that he stayed there for but thirteen years. He then makes the extraordinary statement referred to above—that Leonardo after returning to Florence remained there from 1500 to 1513. Finally he informs us that Leonardo did not die until the year 1542!

I must apologize to my readers for writing at such length as I have done on a writer whose statements regarding Leonardo are, for the most part, a farrago of nonsense. I would not have done so but for the fact that there are art historians today, of the first order, who, by some strange aberration, treat with respect the guesses of this unique historian of the art of painting. A local scribe might be excused had his errors been confined to statements regarding the events in Leonardo's life that had happened in other places than Milan. But his *Succinto Racconto* demonstrates that he was entirely ignorant of the simplest facts regarding Leonardo's periods of residence in that city. It therefore follows that about anything that the artist did or did not do in Milan, he is a witness of no importance.

APPENDIX VI
THE "MONNA LISA"—ADOLFO VENTURI'S THEORY

In support of his theory that the portrait at the Louvre that bears the title "Monna Lisa" is actually the lost portrait of Costanza d'Avalos, the heroine of Ischia, the late Senatore Adolfo Venturi stated that the woman in that picture is represented wearing a widow's veil.[1] This supposition is entirely incorrect. The wife of that wealthy citizen of Florence, Francesco del Giocondo, followed current fashions in her coiffure. She wears no widow's veil.

About the year 1494, when Charles invaded Italy, there appeared in the peninsula a mode of dressing the hair styled "la foggia alla francese," which Italian women believed to be a French fashion.[2] In this style of coiffure, the hair hangs down loosely over the shoulders, and is covered by a veil of gossamer texture, which is held in its place by a narrow ribbon that encircles the head, and that is only visible where it crosses the forehead.

This mode was followed, in their own homes, by leaders of fashion such as Isabella and Beatrice d'Este; though, when they were about to appear at a public function, the sisters were accustomed to have their hair dressed in a much more elaborate style. And it is these more ornate coiffures that we see in contemporary portraits of ceremony.

[1] A. Venturi, *Storia dell'Arte Italiana*, IX, 41.

[2] A. Schiaparelli, *Leonardo Ritrattista* (Milan: Fratelli Treves, 1921).

BIBLIOGRAPHY

ALBERGOTTI, A. *De Vita et Cultu S. Donati Arretinae Ecclesiae Episcopi et Martiris.* Arezzo, 1782.

ALBERTINI, FRANCESCO. *Memoriale di' molte Statue e Picture sono nella inclyta ciptà di Florentia.* Florence, 1510.

AMORETTI, CARLO. *Memorie Storiche sulla Vita di Leonardo da Vinci.* Milan, 1804.

ANONIMO GADDIANO. *Il Codice Magliabecchiano.* Ed. CARL FREY. Berlin, 1892. Also reprinted by C. DE FABRICZY in *Archivio Storico Italiano,* Ser. V, Vol. XII (1893).

BANDELLO, MATTEO. *Novelle.* Lucca, 1554.

BELTRAMI, LUCA. *Documenti e Memorie riguardanti la Vita e le Opere di Leonardo da Vinci.* Milan: Fratelli Treves, 1919.

———. *La Destra Mano di Leonardo.* Milan, 1919.

———. *Il Cenacolo di Leonardo.* Milan, 1908.

BERENSON, B. *The Drawings of the Florentine Painters of the Renaissance.* Chicago: University of Chicago Press, 1938.

———. *The Study and Criticism of Italian Art* [*Third Series*] (London, 1916), pp. 1–27.

———. *Pitture Italiane del Rinascimento.* Milan: Ulrico Hoepli, 1936.

BEUF, C. *Cesare Borgia* (London and New York: Oxford University Press, 1942), pp. 281–85.

BODE, WILHELM VON. "Leonardos Bildnis der jungen Dame mit dem Hermelin aus dem Czartoryski Museum in Krakau, und die Jugenbilder des Kunstlers," *Jahrbuch d. Preuss. Kunstsamml.,* XXXVI (1915), 189–207.

———. *Studien über Leonardo da Vinci.* Berlin, 1921.

———. *Florentine Sculptors of the Renaissance.* New York, 1928.

BODMER, HEINRICH. *Leonardo: Des Meisters Gemälde und Zeichnungen.* "Klassiker der Kunst" Series. Stuttgart, 1931.

BOTTARI, G. G. *Raccolta di Lettere sulla Pittura,* etc. Continuata da STEFANO TICOZZI. Milan: Silvestri, 1822.

BUONAMICO, P. *Discorso sopra la Vita di S. Donato, Vesc. d'Arezzo.* Florence, 1607.

CALVI, G. "Contributi alla Biografia di Leonardo da Vinci," *Archivio Storico Lombardo,* 1916.

———. *I Manoscritti di Leonardo da Vinci, dal punto di visto Cronologico, Storico e Biografico.* Bologna, 1925.

CANUTI, FIORENZO. *Il Perugino.* Siena, 1931.

CARTWRIGHT, JULIA. *Beatrice d'Este.* London: J. M. Dent & Sons, 1899.

CERMANATI, M. "Leonardo in Valtellina," in *Per il Centenario della Morte di Leonardo da Vinci*. Rome: Istituto di Studi Vinciani, 1919.

CHIAPELLI, A. *L'Arte del Rinascimento*. Rome, 1925.

CHIAPELLI, A., and CHITI, A. "Andrea di Verrocchio in Pistoia," *Bollettino Stor. Pistoiese*, Vol. I (1899).

CLARK, KENNETH. *Leonardo da Vinci*. Cambridge: Cambridge University Press, 1939.

———. *A Catalogue of the Drawings of Leonardo da Vinci in the Collection of His Majesty the King, at Windsor Castle*. 2 vols. Cambridge: Cambridge University Press, 1935.

CLAUSSE, G. *Les Sforza e les Arts au Milanais*. Paris: H. Leroux, 1909.

CRUTTWELL, M. *Verrocchio*. London, 1904.

DOUGLAS, R. LANGTON. *Leonardo da Vinci—His San Donato and the Tax Collector*. London: Chiswick Press, 1933.

FENTON, SIR GEOFFREY. *Certaine Tragicall Discourses*. With an Introduction by R. LANGTON DOUGLAS. "Tudor Translation Series." London, 1898.

GAYE, G. *Carteggio inedito d'Artisti*. Florence, 1839, 1840.

GIOVIO, PAOLO. "Leonardo da Vinci, Vita," in TIRABOSCHI, G., *Storia della Letteratura Italiana*, Vol. VII, Part 4. Venice, 1796.

GOLDSCHEIDER, L. *Leonardo da Vinci*. Oxford: Phaidon Press, 1943.

GRONAU, G. *Leonardo da Vinci*. London, 1902.

HORNE, HERBERT P. *The Life of Leonardo da Vinci, by Giorgio Vasari*. London: Longmans, 1903.

LEONARDO DA VINCI. *Trattato della Pittura*. Ed. ANGELO BORZELLI. Lanciano, 1914.

———. *Trattato della Pittura*. German ed. by H. LUDWIG. Vienna, 1882.

LIPMAN, JEAN H. *The Florentine Profile Portrait in the Quattrocento*. Reprinted from the *Art Bulletin*, 1936.

LOMAZZO, G. P. *Trattato dell'arte della Pittura*. Milan, 1584.

LUZIO, A. *I Precettori d'Isabella d'Este*. Ancona, 1887.

———. "Ritratti di Isabella d'Este," *Emporium*, 1900.

McCURDY, E. *Leonardo da Vinci*. London: George Bell & Sons, 1904.

———. *The Mind of Leonardo da Vinci*. London: Cape, 1928.

MALAGUZZI-VALERI, F. *La Corte di Lodovico il Moro*. Milan, 1915.

MARKS, A. *The St. Anne of Leonardo da Vinci*. London, 1894.

MARLE, R. VAN. *Italian Schools of Painting*, Vol. XI. The Hague, 1929.

MATHER, F. J. "Some Recent Leonardo Discoveries," *Art and Archaeology*, 1916, pp. 111 ff.

MILANESI, G. "Documenti inediti riguardanti Leonardo da Vinci," *Archivio Storico Italiano*, Ser. III, Vol. XVI (1872).

MOELLER, E. "Salai und Leonardo da Vinci," *Jahrbuch der Kunsthistorischen Sammlungen in Wien*, N.F., II (1928), 139–61.

MOELLER, E. "Der Geburtstag des Leonardo da Vinci," *Jahrbuch d. Preuss. Kunstsamml.* (1939), pp. 71–75.

MORELLI, G. *Die Galerie zu Berlin*. Leipzig, 1893.

MÜLLER-WALDE, P. *Leonardo da Vinci: Lebenskizze und Forschungen*. Munich, 1889–90.

———. "Beiträge zur Kenntnis des Leonardo da Vinci," *Jahrbuch der Königl. Preuss. Kunstsammlungen* (Berlin, 1897–99).

MÜNTZ, E. *Leonardo da Vinci*. 2 vols. London, 1898.

NICODEMI, G. *Leonardo da Vinci*. Zurich, 1939.

PACIOLI, LUCA. *La Divina Proportione*. Venice, 1509.

PANOFSKY, E. *The Codex Huygens and Leonardo da Vinci's Art Theory*. "Studies of the Warburg Institute," Vol. XIII. London, 1940.

PASTOR, L. *Die Reise des Cardinals Luigi d'Aragona*. Freiburg-i-B., 1905.

PATER, W. H. *The Renaissance*. London, 1893.

POGGI, G. *Leonardo da Vinci, La Vita di Giorgio Vasari Nuovamente Commentata e Illustrata*, etc. Florence, 1919.

RAMUSIO, G. B. *Primo Volume delle Navigazioni e Viaggi*, etc. Venice, 1850.

RATTI, ACHILLE (POPE PIUS XI). "Ancora della 'Sacra Famiglia' di Bernardino Luini all'Ambrosiana," *Rassegna d'Arte*, 1912.

REBER, FRANZ VON, and BAYERSDORFER, AD. *Klassischer Bilderschatz*. Munich, n.d.

REINACH, S. "La Tristesse di Mona Lisa," *Bulletin des Musées de France*. Paris, 1909.

RICHTER, G. M. "A Leonardo Profile," *Art in America*, July, 1941.

RICHTER, J. P., and IRMA A. *The Literary Works of Leonardo da Vinci*. 2 vols. 2d ed. London and New York: Oxford University Press, 1939.

RINALDIS, ALDO DE. *Storia dell'Opera Pittorica di Leonardo da Vinci*. Bologna: Zanichelli, 1926.

SABBA DA CASTIGLIONE. *Ricordi overo ammaestramenti*. Venice, 1554.

SCHIAPARELLI, A. *Leonardo Ritrattista*. Milan: Treves, 1921.

SÉAILLES, G. *Léonard de Vinci, l'Artiste et le Savant*. Paris, 1892.

SEIDLITZ, WALDEMAR VON. *Leonardo da Vinci, der Wendepunkt der Renaissance*. 2 vols. Berlin, 1909. 2d ed., enlarged. Vienna: Phaidon-Verlag, 1935.

SIRÉN, O. *Leonardo da Vinci, The Artist and the Man*. London and New Haven: Yale University Press, 1916.

SMIRAGLIA-SCOGNAMIGLIO, N. *Ricerche e Documenti sulla Giovinezza di Leonardo da Vinci*. Naples, 1900.

SOLMI, E. *Leonardo*. Florence, 1900.

———. "Le Fonti dei Manoscritti di Leonardo da Vinci," *Giornale Storico della Letteratura Italiana*. Turin, 1908.

SUIDA, WILHELM. *Leonardo und sein Kreis*. Munich, 1929.

———. "A Leonardo Profile and Dynamism in Art," *Art in America*, April, 1941.

Surius, F. R. Laurentius. *De Probatis Sanctorum Vitis*. Cologne, 1618.

Thiis, Jens. *Leonardo da Vinci: The Florentine Years of Leonardo and Verrocchio*. London, n.d. [?1913].

Uzielli, G. *Ricerche intorno a Leonardo da Vinci, Albero genealogico della Famiglia Vinci*. Florence, 1872; Rome, 1884.

Valentiner, W. R. "Leonardo as Verrocchio's Co-worker," *Art Bulletin*, March, 1930, p. 43.

———. "Leonardo's Portrait of Beatrice d'Este," *Art in America*, January, 1937.

Vasari, G. *Le Vite*. Ed. G. Milanesi. Florence: Sansoni, 1878–85.

Venturi, A. *Storia dell'arte Italiana*, Vol. IX. Milan, 1925.

———. *Leonardo da Vinci*. "Pubblicazioni dell'Istituto di Studii Vinciani in Roma," Vol. II. Bologna, 1920.

———. "L'Uso della Mano Sinistra nella scrittura e nei disegni di Leonardo da Vinci," *L'Arte*, 1939, pp. 167–73.

Venturi, L. *La Critica e l'arte di Leonardo da Vinci*. "Pubblicazioni dell'Istituto di Studi Vinciani in Roma." Bologna, 1919.

Verga, Ettore. *Raccolta Vinciana presso l'Archivio Storico del Commune di Milano*, 1903 and after.

———. *Bibliografia Vinciana, 1491–1930*. 2 vols. Bologna, 1931.

Yriarte, C. "Les Relations d'Isabella d'Este avec Léonard de Vinci," *Gazette des Beaux Arts*, Vol. XXXVII. Paris, 1888.

INDEX

PLATES

PLATE II

LEONARDO DA VINCI. ANGELS, A DETAIL FROM
VERROCCHIO'S BAPTISM. UFFIZI, FLORENCE

PLATE III

Leonardo

LEONARDO DA VINCI. THE VAL D'ARNO, A DRAWING, 1473. UFFIZI, FLORENCE

PLATE IV

LEONARDO DA VINCI. A STORM IN THE ALPS, A DRAWING
WINDSOR CASTLE, NO. 12.409

PLATE V

LEONARDO DA VINCI. ALPINE LANDSCAPE, A DRAWING
WINDSOR CASTLE, NO. 12.408

PLATE VI

LEONARDO DA VINCI. CHIAVENNA, A DRAWING. WINDSOR CASTLE, NO. 12.399

PLATE VII

LEONARDO DA VINCI. ISABELLA D'ESTE, A CARTOON
1499, 1500. LOUVRE, PARIS

PLATE VIII

ANDREA DEL BRESCIANINO. THE VIRGIN AND CHILD AND ST. ANNE. BERLIN

PLATE IX

LEONARDO DA VINCI. MADONNA AND CHILD. DREYFUS COLLECTION, PARIS

PLATE X

LEONARDO DA VINCI. MADONNA AND CHILD, A DETAIL
DREYFUS COLLECTION, PARIS

PLATE XI

PLATE XII

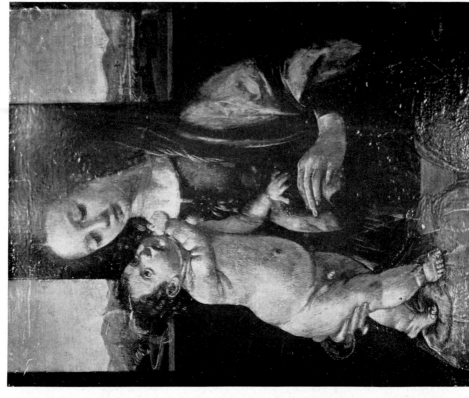

LEONARDO DA VINCI. MADONNA AND CHILD, AN ULTRA-VIOLET-
RAY PHOTOGRAPH. DREYFUS COLLECTION, PARIS

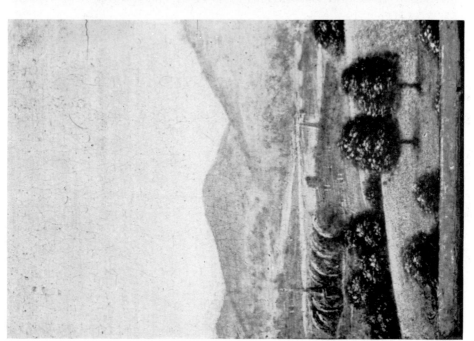

LEONARDO DA VINCI. MADONNA AND CHILD
A DETAIL. DREYFUS COLLECTION, PARIS

PLATE XIII

LEONARDO DA VINCI AND DOMENICO GHIRLANDAJO. THE ANNUNCIATION. UFFIZI, FLORENCE

PLATE XIV

LEONARDO DA VINCI. GINEVRA DEI BENCI. LIECHTEN-
STEIN COLLECTION, VIENNA

PLATE XV

ANDREA DEL VERROCCHIO. THE MADONNA DI PIAZZA
CATHEDRAL, PISTOIA

PLATE XVI

PERUGINO. THE BIRTH OF ST. JOHN THE BAPTIST, 1477. WALKER ART GALLERY, LIVERPOOL

LEONARDO DA VINCI. THE ANNUNCIATION. LOUVRE, PARIS

PLATE XVIII

LORENZO DI CREDI. THE ANNUNCIATION. UFFIZI, FLORENCE

PLATE XIX

LEONARDO DA VINCI. A STUDY FOR DRAPERY. WINDSOR CASTLE, NO. 12.521

PLATE XX

LEONARDO DA VINCI. SAN DONATO AND THE TAX COLLECTOR
WORCESTER ART MUSEUM, WORCESTER, MASSACHUSETTS

PLATE XXI

SCHOOL OF ANDREA DEL VERROCCHIO. MADONNA
A DRAWING. DRESDEN GALLERY

PLATE XXII

LEONARDO DA VINCI. MADONNA AND CHILD. ALTE PINAKOTHEK, MUNICH

PLATE XXIII

LEONARDO DA VINCI. THE BENOIS MADONNA. THE HERMITAGE, LENINGRAD

PLATE XXV

LEONARDO DA VINCI. THE MADONNA OF THE
CAT, A DRAWING. BRITISH MUSEUM
LONDON

PLATE XXIV

LEONARDO DA VINCI. MADONNA AND CHILD, A
STUDY FOR THE BENOIS MADONNA
LOUVRE, PARIS

PLATE XXVI

LEONARDO DA VINCI. ADORATION OF THE MAGI, 1481–82. UFFIZI, FLORENCE

PLATE XXVII

LEONARDO DA VINCI. THE ADORATION OF THE MAGI, A DRAWING
GALLICHON COLLECTION, LOUVRE, PARIS

PLATE XXVIII

LEONARDO DA VINCI. THE ADORATION OF THE MAGI, A DETAIL
UFFIZI, FLORENCE

PLATE XXIX

LEONARDO DA VINCI. ST. JEROME. VATICAN GALLERY

PLATE XXX

LEONARDO DA VINCI. THE VIRGIN OF THE ROCKS. LOUVRE, PARIS

PLATE XXXI

LEONARDO DA VINCI. STUDY FOR A NATIVITY
METROPOLITAN MUSEUM, NEW YORK

PLATE XXXII

LEONARDO DA VINCI. THE VIRGIN OF THE ROCKS, A DETAIL. LOUVRE, PARIS

PLATE XXXIII

LEONARDO DA VINCI. THE VIRGIN OF THE ROCKS, A DETAIL. LOUVRE, PARIS

PLATE XXXIV

LEONARDO DA VINCI. BEATRICE D'ESTE. CASTEL-PIZZUTO COLLECTION, MILAN

PLATE XXXV

GIAN CRISTOFORO ROMANO. BEATRICE D'ESTE, A MARBLE BUST. LOUVRE, PARIS

PLATE XXXVI

MILANESE ARTIST. BEATRICE D'ESTE, AN
ILLUMINATED MANUSCRIPT, ACT OF
DONATION. BRITISH MUSEUM

PLATE XXXVII

MILANESE COIN OF 1496
BEATRICE D'ESTE

PLATE XXXVIII

SCHOOL OF FERRARA. BEATRICE AND ISABELLA D'ESTE, A FRESCO
PALAZZO COSTABILI, FERRARA

PLATE XXXIX

SCHOOL OF MILAN. BEATRICE D'ESTE. CASTELLO SFORZESCO, MILAN

PLATE XL

LORENZO COSTA. LA COUR D'ISABELLA D'ESTE. LOUVRE, PARIS

PLATE XLI

LEONARDO DA VINCI. CECILIA GALLERANI. CZARTORYSKI MUSEUM, CRACOW

PLATE XLII

LEONARDO DA VINCI. PORTRAIT OF A MUSICIAN
BIBLIOTECA AMBROSIANA, MILAN

PLATE XLIII

LEONARDO DA VINCI AND BOLTRAFFIO. LA BELLE FERRONIÈRE. LOUVRE, PARIS

PLATE XLIV

MARCO D'OGGIONO. PORTRAIT OF A LADY AS VENUS
LEDERER COLLECTION, VIENNA

PLATE XLV

LEONARDO DA VINCI. THE LAST SUPPER, 1496-98. SANTA MARIA DELLE GRAZIE, MILAN

PLATE XLVI

MARCO D'OGGIONO. THE LAST SUPPER, COPY AFTER LEONARDO. LOUVRE, PARIS

PLATE XLVII

GIOVANNI FRANCESCO MELZI. VERTUMNUS AND POMONA
KAISER FRIEDRICH MUSEUM, BERLIN

PLATE XLVIII

B. LUINI. THE MADONNA WITH THE YARN-WINDER, COPY AFTER LOST
LEONARDO. LOCKER-LAMPSON COLLECTION, LONDON

PLATE XLIX

LEONARDO DA VINCI. MONNA LISA, A CARTOON
COLLECTION OF BARON VITTA, PARIS

PLATE L

LEONARDO DA VINCI. A LILY, A DRAWING
WINDSOR CASTLE, NO. 12.418

PLATE LI

LEONARDO DA VINCI. MONNA LISA, 1500–1505. LOUVRE, PARIS

PLATE LII

LEONARDO DA VINCI. MONNA LISA, LANDSCAPE
A DETAIL. LOUVRE, PARIS

PLATE LIV

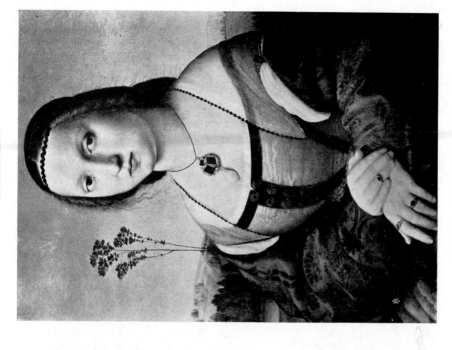

RAPHAEL. MADDALENA DONI, 1506
PITTI GALLERY, FLORENCE

PLATE LIII

RAPHAEL. PORTRAIT OF A WOMAN, A DRAWING
LOUVRE, PARIS

PLATE LV

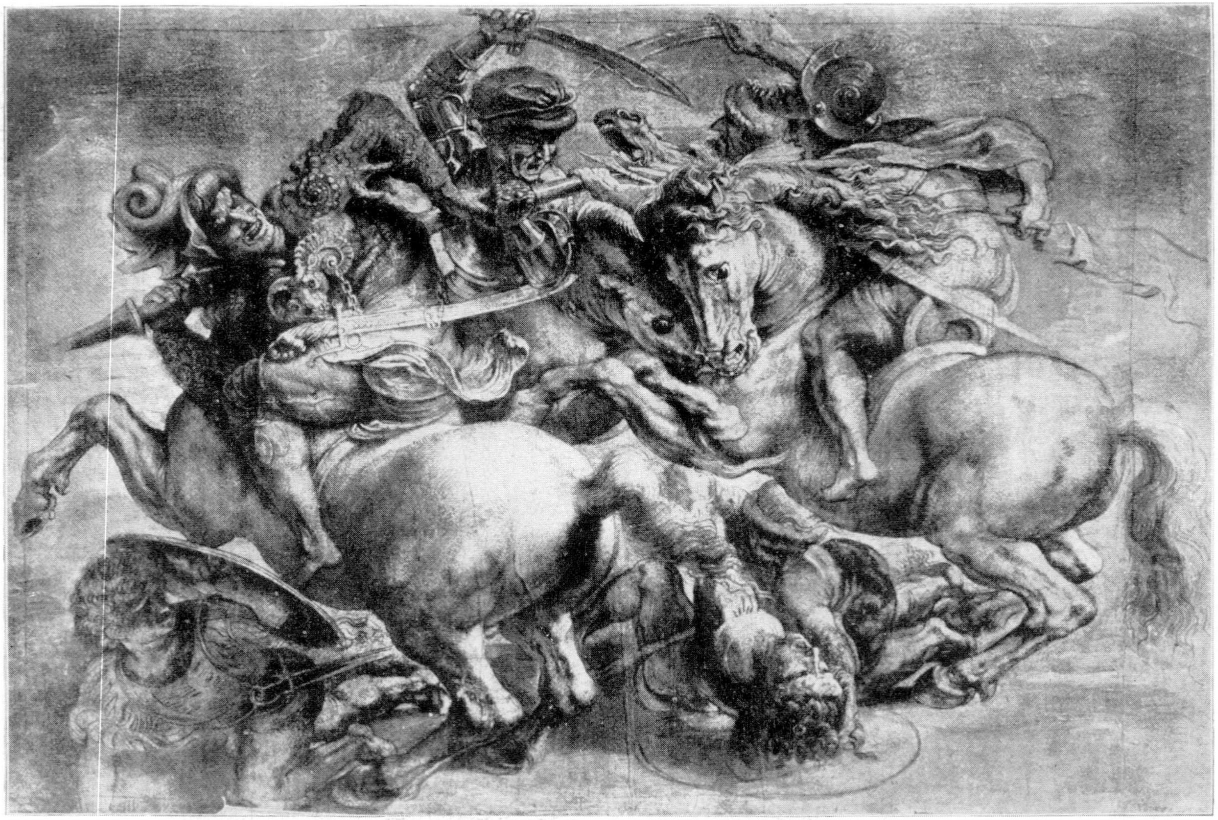

SIR P. P. RUBENS. THE BATTLE OF THE STANDARD, COPY OF A PART OF THE BATTLE OF ANGHIARI. LOUVRE, PARIS

PLATE LVI

LEONARDO DA VINCI AND AN ASSISTANT. VIRGIN AND CHILD
AND ST. ANNE. LOUVRE, PARIS

PLATE LVII

LEONARDO DA VINCI. ST. JOHN THE BAPTIST. LOUVRE, PARIS